Mrs. Rowe's

Restaurant Cookbook

Mrs. Rowe's Restaurant Cookbook

A Lifetime of Recipes from the Shenandoah Valley

Mollie Cox Bryan &
Mrs. Rowe's Family Restaurant

TEN SPEED PRESS
Berkeley | Toronto

Dedicated in memory of

Mildred Craft Rowe, 1912–2003

With much honor and gratitude to Virginia Bowers and Bertha Mays, her sisters.
And to all of Mildred's family, in whom her legacy grows and thrives.
Also dedicated to Eric Bryan and Michael DiGrassie, who have both
made all things possible, in very different ways.

Ten Speed Press
Box 7123
Berkeley, California 94707
www.tenspeed.com

Distributed in Australia by Simon and Schuster Australia, in Canada by Ten Speed Press Canada, in New Zealand by Southern Publishers Group, in South Africa by Real Books, and in the United Kingdom and Europe by Publishers Group UK.

Design by Kate Basart/Union Pageworks

Library of Congress Cataloging-in-Publication Data

Bryan, Mollie Cox, 1963–
    The Mrs. Rowe Family Restaurant cookbook : a lifetime of recipes from the
Shenandoah Valley / Mollie Cox Bryan and the Mrs. Rowe's Family Restaurant.
        p. cm.
    Includes bibliographical references and index.
    ISBN-13: 978-1-58008-734-6 (alk. paper)
    ISBN-10: 1-58008-734-5 (alk. paper)
    1. Cookery, American—Southern style. 2. Mrs. Rowe Family Restaurant. I. Mrs. Rowe Family Restaurant.
II. Title.
    TX715.2.S68B79 2006
    641.5975—dc222006013822

Printed in China
First printing, 2006
1 2 3 4 5 6 7 8 9 10 — 10 09 08 07 06

Contents

Foreword ix
Acknowledgments xi
Introduction xiii

1 Biscuits, Bread & Breakfast Treats
Kicking the Dirt off Corn   1

2 Sauces, Gravies & Preserves
You Can Take the Girl Out of the Farm...   19

3 Salads, Dressings & Relishes
When One Door Closes...   39

4 Soups & Stews
Goshen Days and Blackberries Like Gold   63

5 Sides
"Skillet," the Man from Staunton   81

6 Main Dishes
Making Staunton Home   105

7 Pie
Culinary Life Force   137

8 Cakes
Growing Pains   163

9 Other Desserts
Ever After   183

10 Epilogue
Gone, but Not Forgotten   201

Index 207

Foreword

Over half a century ago, Alan Lomax traveled through the South discovering blues music and musicians, documenting an American folk art. In recent years, the same process has taken place in the world of food. Hitherto unrecognized cooks in humble restaurants all around the country have been discovered and celebrated as masters of America's folk cuisine. One of the brightest landmarks in that recognition is Mollie Bryan's book about the indomitable Mrs. Rowe. Here are a woman and a restaurant and a canon of recipes that epitomize eating, country style.

We first came across Mrs. Rowe's place by accident. Traveling along Route 81 through Virginia, we got off the highway when hunger struck; frankly, we were not all that excited by the sight of what was then called The Rowe Family Restaurant. It looked like hundreds of other eateries at the ends of highway ramps. But the smell of warm sticky buns just inside the front door told another story. We've been back to Mrs. Rowe's many times over the years, and while the pork chops and fried chicken have always been truly memorable, our favorite memory is the time we interviewed Mrs. Milred Rowe for *Gourmet* magazine. While we were sitting in the dining room chatting about her upbringing in the hills of Alleghany County, a waitress walked past with a tray that included a small bowl of macaroni and cheese, one of about a dozen "vegetables" on the menu every day. "Ooo, look!" Mildred said, her attention magnetically drawn away from conversation to the mound of baked golden-orange noodles venting buttery steam and laced with chewy shreds of cheese. "Macaroni and cheese!" she exclaimed like a thirsty oenophile observing the uncorking of a bottle of 1959 Lafite Rothschild. "Doesn't that look good?"

Her passion for the mac 'n' cheese was repeated in virtually all that happened in her restaurant. Nothing escaped her insistence on cooking everything right, and serving it graciously too. Only a few years before our interview, she had changed the name of her establishment to Mrs. Rowe's Restaurant, cutting out the word *family* because of the dubious connotations it has assumed in the restaurant business. She and her son Michael explained that too often *family* now meant a menu of quick-fix meals, sandwiches, and hamburgers, or a sloppy buffet where you had to fight with other customers to get your food. When Mrs. Rowe had named her place a family restaurant years before, she was expressing a degree of civility as well as the sort of food that American families in the South have traditionally gathered around a table to share.

Mrs. Rowe's insistence on the old ways of cooking and serving meals became more and more of anomaly for an interstate restaurant, especially in the days of Cracker Barrel and other big franchises. And yet in her hands, and in the hands of her progeny, it has remained utterly unspoiled. There have always been plenty of people who appreciate the food and the grace, filling the restaurant's big dining rooms every day of the year except Thanksgiving, Christmas, New Year's Day, and the Fourth of July (when it is closed so employees can spend the holidays together with their families).

The devotion of some customers is legendary. Many years ago, a pregnant woman went into labor but refused to leave her table until she could eat some fried chicken. Mrs. Rowe's chicken, skillet-cooked to order, demands a thirty-five minute wait. The result is spectacularly tasty: brittle red-gold skin with a savory crunch hugging moist meat tender as butter. Mrs. Rowe took matters into her own hands, escorted the young woman to her car, and drove her to the emergency room. Years later, the woman brought her child back for her daughter's birthday and they both finally got their fried chicken.

Back in the early 1980s, Mike wrote to thank us for including the restaurant in an early edition of our guidebook, *Roadfood*. In his letter, he noted, "So many travelers are in despair. Fast food has been putting all the good places out of business. But we feel the trend has been reversed and good food is due for a large scale revival."

He was right. There is plenty of fast food wherever you go, but that doesn't mean that cooking with character is gone. Institutional burger joints are fine in their predictable sort of way, but they could never take the place of the authentic barbecues, oyster bars, and catfish parlors that can make eating one's way across America a delectable adventure. Any time you need reassurance about that fact, you can stop at Mrs. Rowe's place for pork chops, candied yams, and baked apples; or equally as satisfying, simply read through, or cook from, this book, which is a treasure trove of her legacy.

—JANE AND MICHAEL STERN, AUTHORS OF *Roadfood*

Acknowledgments

First, I want to thank my daughters, Emma and Tess, who have been through more sitters than I ever could have imagined during the four years or so of writing and rewriting of this book. A thank you goes to my husband, Eric, for his steadfast, enduring commitment and support. This book is a real culmination of our family effort.

This book is also the culmination of the efforts of many Mrs. Rowe's family members, starting with her oldest daughter, Brenda Hathaway. She gathered, tested, and developed the recipes in the restaurant's self-published cookbook, which has sold more than eighty-thousand copies. A large portion of those recipes is contained in this book, along with recipes never before published, some contributed by other family members. A special note of gratitude goes to Brenda for her hard work on the first book.

Thanks the DiGrassie-Rowe family, especially Mike, Brenda, Linda, and Ginger who put up with my personal questions and prying nature. Mary Lou DiGrassie also must be thanked for her time, efforts, and memories. Terry LeMasurier, Ginger's husband, offered a unique point of view, for which I am grateful. Also, because of Mrs. Rowe's health problems, I relied on the memories of her two sisters Bertha Mays and Virginia Bowers, now passed away. Carroll Mays, Mrs. Rowe's nephew, was also a treasure trove of information. I also spoke with some of Mildred's grandchildren—Aaron, Wynne, Anne, and Sarah, and I thank them for their time and efforts. Also, many family members in Covington and Rich Patch were gracious, hospitable, friendly, and helpful.

I also found several local history folks and researchers to be very helpful. Ina McAllister, Covington Historical Society, The Homestead, Staunton Downtown Development Association, and the Food History Timeline.

In addition, several locals and employees of Rowe's offered their memories and impressions of Mrs. Rowe. They are: Fred Brown, Marion and Jean Harner, Frances Clemmer, Dot Woodrum, Tootie McLear, Betsy Fultz, Roger and Sonie Bible, Gladys Austin, Vivian Obie, Edgar Walker, Mary-Lydia Graham, Oliver Hildebrand, Judy Hatcher, Agnes Davis, Lorraine Thompson, Carroll Lisle, Phil Grasty, Don Sheets, Bonnie Cash, Sally Rowe, Blanche Wimer Probst, Marion Robertson, Mary Brown, Carole Hinton, Lura McCulty, Janis and Edie Jaquith. I hope I have not forgotten anyone.

Several friends reviewed the manuscript and proposal at different points in the process: Jennifer Neisslein, Robin Bryan, Peggy Sheets, Yvonne Feeley, Nicole Oeschlin, Alice Leonhardt, Logan Ward, the Blue Ridge Community College Writer's Group, and my husband Eric, who has read this book so many times that he can probably recite it word for word by now.

I also owe extreme gratitude to Bella Stander who told me about Lisa Ekus, a literary agent of great generosity who telephoned me and pointed me in the absolute right direction—to my current agent, Angela Miller, who never gave up hope.

Thanks to several friends and family members for moral support (some of whom are mentioned already in the previous list): Sandy Cox, Charles Cox, Shirley Cox, Becky Gay, Abbey and Carly Wamboldt, Andi Minteer, Susan Pereles, Jennifer Ledford, Kevin Shirley, Kate Antea, Dawn Woodrum, Fran Marylis, Kathy Cheeks, Reid Oeschlin, Bob and Betty Bryan, and Margaret Flather.

I also must thank the folks I met at the National Food Writers Symposium at the Greenbrier a few years ago, Don Fry, Sheri Castle, Lynn Swann, and Antonia Allegra, as they have all been helpful at various points during this book project.

A very special thanks goes to Michael Stern, who generously read the whole, big, biography in a very raw form. His words of support have inspired me throughout this project.

I was most assuredly blessed with a dream of an editor, Lily Binns. I am grateful her hard work, patience, and thoughtful, intelligent feedback. Also, thanks to photographer Ed Anderson, art director Nancy Austin, copyeditor Holly Taines White, and the whole magnificent Ten Speed team.

Many thanks to you all.

—Mollie

Introduction

"Success in feeding people can only be measured, ultimately, by the lives that are touched and the quality of that touch."

—PETER REINHART, *Sacramental Magic in a Small-Town Cafe*

Throughout the morning, eggs, ham, freshly baked biscuits, and, of course, never-ending pots of coffee fill tables and counters at Mrs. Rowe's Restaurant and Bakery in Staunton, Virginia. Dishes and cups clank, spoons stir cream and sugar. A laugh rings out, along with a familiar "How-do." A customer walks in and shouts across the counter: "You got them ham biscuits today?" The waitress smiles and nods: "Sure do."

On this particular day in June 2002, I sat across the table from Mrs. Rowe herself, the woman who jump-started the then fifty-five-year-old, family-run business. As she spoke, her hands were in constant motion. She moved cups and plates around to see if we needed more coffee, more breakfast. These gestures were ingrained and second nature for her. Her hands seemed to have a life of their own.

"I love this place," she said, taking it all in, with pride. Her eyes filled with tears.

Mildred Rowe was a bit emotional that day. She had suffered a heart attack and had been away from the restaurant for a while. She was dressed, as always, impeccably and appropriately for a prosperous but unassuming Southern woman of a certain age and status. She wore a

A young Mildred, proud of her prizewinning potato crop.

The old Dark Hollow Baptist Church, where the Craft family attended services.

crisp pink shirt with a floral patterned jacket and a little lipstick and rouge. Her white hair was perfectly coiffed.

She was eighty-nine years old. And as she looked around her place—a restaurant that has become legendary with those who travel the I-81 corridor in Virginia—the love and pride on her face and in her eyes was clear. The story of how she came to this place and time is long and fascinating.

The food at Mrs. Rowe's is home-style, Appalachian, Southern cooking at affordable prices. Some folks have been eating breakfast at the restaurant every morning for twenty years, or every Sunday for fifteen. Many look forward to at least one weekly meal and some locals eat there for every meal, every day.

Marion and Jean Harner ate at Rowe's every day for fifteen years—sometimes twice a day. "In all that time, I never had to send anything back," says Jean.

"When I came back to Staunton, I had been cooking in places like Italy and Arizona. When I walked into Moo's (that's what I call my grandmother) restaurant, I had whole sense of respect for what she had done with her life and with this place. I saw connections between her food and the food in Italy and France, for example. I decided to stay here because I thought I could not find a better teacher anywhere. Her knowledge of food was so vast."

—Aaron DiGrassie, Mildred's grandson

Many of Rowe's customers, like the Harners, are not interested in the national inclination for low-fat and low-carb food or the fact that 30 percent of Americans eat four meatless meals per week. Rowe's has a meat-based menu with hardly anything low-fat, low-carb, or vegetarian, though the restaurant is offering more and more options each year.

But there is something more than the menu to this place. More than the food. There has to be when considering a business that is so incredibly successful. Yes, lots of people will cite the food as being the reason they come, but many more will tell you it was Mrs. Rowe herself that brought them in. Her sassy personality and reputation for perfection attract customers, and they keep coming back.

Even now, after her death, a strong, feisty, grandmotherly presence is felt. Starting with the barn-red, white-trimmed exterior and the petunias and azaleas lining the sidewalk and entrance way, customers sense an immaculate, feminine, welcoming presence. Chairs line the front room that resembles a sun porch, reminding customers, perhaps, of their own homes. The room is filled with framed magazine and newspaper articles about the restaurant, with photos of a grinning Mrs. Rowe. Customers know, indeed, whose place this is.

"*I remember the first time a black man came into the Goshen restaurant. Aunt Millie said that she was sorry, but she could not serve him. She worried that her other customers might take offense at seeing a black man eating there. But it bothered her. That was when she and Mom made up their minds they would begin to serve blacks, which was a brave, if not visionary, move on their part. I mean, this was about 1948.*"

—CARROLL MAYS, MILDRED'S NEPHEW

Inside, most of the walls are paneled to be woodsy and cozy, though the panels in the front section are painted creamy white to set off the dark green chair cushions and booth seats. The walls are decorated with soothing country landscapes and an antique English sleeping bench greets customers, along with the always-friendly staff.

Off to the left in the front room sits a now-empty rocking chair. Is she really gone? Mildred Rowe's vision for and ultimate creation of this place are living things. Palpable. Her passion filled this restaurant so full that it brims with a soothing magnetism.

Comfort is the best way to sum up the kind of food and feeling one gets from Rowe's. Most Americans dine out for more than convenience and hunger. It is the experience—the feeling—that they are craving. If the success of this restaurant is any indication, then one of the things cynical, world-weary Americans long for is pure and simple comfort. The kind we get from our mothers' and grandmothers' kitchens.

And so we are back to Mildred, mother of four, grandmother of eleven, a farm girl who grew up during the Depression, a young woman who worked in butcher shops and factories, who found her way into two restaurant businesses—one of which is now a multimillion-dollar operation serving half a million meals a year.

As a child growing up in the mountains of Virginia, could Mildred have dreamed such a life? As she was walking, often barefoot, three miles along a dirt road to her one-room school with her brothers and sisters, what did she think about her future? As she trekked the few miles through the fields and dust to Dark Hollow Baptist Church every Sunday, did she think of the rewards that would come her way from living a good Christian life?

The answers to these questions provide fodder for the mystery of any life. But given Mildred's time and circumstances, it is safe to say that she could never have dreamed her life as it turned out. Rich Patch, Virginia, was isolated and so she had probably never heard of restaurants until she moved from the mountain. Even then, restaurants were rare.

Her joys were simple. She thrived when she had her hands in the earth and took great pride in its bounty, which must have seemed miraculous enough. Having eleven brothers and sisters, Mildred developed a sense of competition. She raced to pick the most potatoes and wanted to grow the biggest and the best of anything. Her sense of competition was not the only reason she worked so hard. She loved to work perhaps because of the sense of accomplishment, or perhaps it was sparked by her Baptist faith. Or it may have been the simple fact that Mildred liked to be on the move.

Later, in her early twenties, when she moved to the town of Covington and worked in factories, she held firmly to her happy work ethic. She also held firmly to the food she had grown to love, which prompted her to have her own garden—no matter where she lived. In Covington, she found that she learned any job quickly, would excel at it, then get bored and need to move on. This must have been a confidence booster. Young women of that era were not often told that they could do what they wanted with their lives, or that they were capable of anything other than raising children, feeding the family, and keeping a clean house. Although Mildred had never really wanted to leave the mountain, she could, perhaps, see now that there was more to life than her farm.

When she married Eugene DiGrassie in May of 1934, she still worked intermittently. It was as if she struggled with her role as a wife. She didn't give in when Eugene asked her to stay home, as most women did at the time. Later, when her marriage with Eugene fell apart, Mildred was able to call on her love of work and her finely developed sense of business to help her and her three children survive.

Though Mildred did not sit around and feel sorry for herself, her divorce deeply troubled her. She had no role models, having never known anybody who divorced. There were no magazines with glossy "healing from divorce" headlines, no Oprah Winfreys beckoning from the television, no support groups, and no welfare. Growing up on the mountain, marriage was a stabilizing, permanent force. Once married, that was it, come hell or high water.

This was a confusing and painful time for Mildred as she struggled to find her way. Her family, with their strong bond, stepped in and helped her out. But she also found that work was a great healer. She embarked on a restaurant business in Goshen, Virginia. She had to make it work—and she did. She rolled up her sleeves and got down to business. Her soon busy restaurant in Goshen did not allow her to dwell on her failed marriage.

Even though Mildred did not like to discuss this time period in her life, it affected her future in profound ways. Not only did she learn the business that would eventually make her famous, but she also discovered more about herself than she would have had she stayed married to DiGrassie. She became a whole and confident, though wounded, person.

The night line crew at Mrs. Rowe's Restaurant and Bakery today.

Fast Facts about Mrs. Rowe's Restaurant and Bakery

On Mother's Day, May 11, 2003, Mrs. Rowe's sold more than 4,000 meals.

The restaurant sells more than half a million meals a year, including:

* 22,000 pies
* 36,500 dozen homemade rolls
* 60,000 pounds of potatoes
* 34,000 pounds of chicken
* 12,750 loaves of homemade bread
* 40,000 dozen eggs
* 8,150 pounds of pork tenderloin
* 25,000 pounds of hamburger

It was the first restaurant in the area to go completely nonsmoking.

It is the only local restaurant to be written up in *Gourmet* and *Travel & Leisure*. It has also been written about in more than 250 newspapers and has been featured in *BackRoads USA* and *GRIT* magazines.

The restaurant's self-published cookbook, *Mrs. Rowe's Favorite Recipes*, has sold 80,000 copies and continues to sell at a rate of at least 100 a week. This is without any marketing effort and it is only sold at the restaurant and two local gift shops.

The restaurant has been in business and owned by the same family since 1947. As such, it is the most successful family-owned and -operated restaurant in the state of Virginia.

About 10 percent of the restaurant's profits come from an average of 4,000 frozen entrées sales a month.

Happy Baby, Happy Mother

Sissy Hutching-Mass had been going to the restaurant all of her life. When she brought her new baby in, he was fussing and fussing. Mildred picked him up and he stopped crying. "I'll tell you what," she said. "I want you to enjoy your meal. Let me take him in the back. You come and get him when you're ready."

When Sissy finished eating, she found Mildred and the baby asleep in Mildred's rocking chair in the office. "I just couldn't believe it. There was my fussy baby, asleep with Mrs. Rowe," says Sissy, voice cracking.

The universe was conspiring in her success. Her time on the farm, followed by the years of factory work, and then experience in local businesses, gave her basic skills and knowledge. All this, mixed with the emotional wherewithal she gathered during her divorce, led her to a new level of understanding about her life. She had not planned any of this. She made the most of the opportunities offered to her and forged a future with her hands, feet, and extraordinary sense of taste.

Her astounding success in Goshen drew more and more people into the eatery; one of these people would help change her life again. This person was attracted by her beauty, absolutely, but also by the strong, independent, smart woman Mildred Craft DiGrassie had become. That person was Willard Rowe, a man who was struggling with his own restaurant in Staunton, Virginia.

Once again, the universe appeared to be conspiring. Call it karma or kismet or the answer to a prayer. Willard and Mildred fell in love, got married, and she moved to Staunton to help save his business.

Willard no doubt saw in Mildred a successful businessperson with an interesting combination of qualities. She was an anomaly, a curiosity to women and to men. In the six short years she was in Goshen, she was a financial success. She not only paid off her business loan for the restaurant, but she also had plenty of money in the bank and had become a vital part of the town.

For a woman to do so well on her own was extraordinary during that time. Most women were raising families and working at home. Annie Hinkle, Mildred's Goshen neighbor, is a fine contemporary example. She was smart, raised her family,

Most Popular Entrées

Hamburger Steak
Baked Pork Tenderloin
Fried Chicken
Stuffed Peppers
Fried Catfish
Chicken-Fried Steak
Country-Style Steak

Most Popular Lunch Orders

Chicken Salad Sandwich
Homemade Vegetable Beef Soup

Most Popular Side Order

Spoon Bread

Most Ordered Desserts

Coconut Cream Pie
Banana Pudding

and kept her house. "It certainly would not have occurred to me to own and operate my own business," says Annie.

Mildred's finances had improved so much that she was even extended credit to buy a washer from Sears. Most credit applications did not have a space for an unmarried woman on their forms. Everything was geared for men or married women, who often had to get their husband's signature as permission to get a job, obtain a driver's license, open a bank account, and so on. Mildred navigated the situation and enjoyed her washer—making sure she never missed the $3 payment every Saturday.

Mildred did not just do well by her family, though. She always believed that a successful business owner should give back to the community, but she was not one for setting up foundations. She just offered a helping hand when she could, such as shutting down the restaurant to feed a family whose father had died.

Mrs. Rowe's Top Ten Restaurant Business Rules

1. Clean. And clean again.
2. Treat customers like family.
3. Don't be afraid of the competition, it can only make you better.
4. Don't serve alcohol without a meal.
5. If you consistently have lines of people waiting to get in, your prices are too low.
6. Keep it simple.
7. Keep it fresh and real. (Real mashed potatoes; real meat; local, fresh produce; and so on.)
8. Every penny counts, so count every penny.
9. Close at a decent hour (8 P.M., sharp.)
10. Be there. "You've got to be there to keep an eye on things," she often said.

Mildred once drove an unmarried woman with a new baby home to her family in Roanoke, a distance of about ninety miles. The woman had gotten off at the bus stop in front of the restaurant. She had no money and didn't know what she was going to do. Mildred closed the restaurant in the middle of the day and drove her to her parents' house.

Whether it was her Baptist faith or her own heartbreak that made her sensitive to the plight of others, it's hard to say. The stories of her compassion have become a part of her legend. Anecdotes about this prosperous woman doing good for others showed the locals that she was not a self-centered, greedy businesswoman. She was kindhearted.

Some of her customers became protective of that heart and were even concerned in the 1960s when Mildred would feed hippies hitchhiking through Staunton. Sometimes she took them home to get cleaned up and to sleep in a warm bed. "If a person is hungry, feed them," she often said. This philosophy still informs operations of her restaurant.

Some of the stories about the restaurant and Mildred have become national legend as well. Sometimes, more than one version exists. For example, Jane and Michael Stern tell one version of the pregnant woman and fried chicken story in their foreword. But there is another one.

IF YOU LIKE OUR FOOD TELL OTHERS
- IF NOT TELL US.

The pregnant woman craved Mildred's fried chicken. As luck would have it, she went into labor before the meal was brought to her table. She called from the hospital, "I want that chicken so bad." Mildred took the chicken to her while she was in labor. Going above and beyond what was expected of her as a restaurant owner was another piece of the secret to Mildred's success.

Part of a business's reputation is its product, part is its role in the community, and another vital part is how employees are treated. Because Mildred and Willard both worked hard, they expected the same from their employees. Mildred was very particular about the way the food tasted—and the way it looked. She sent many plates back to the kitchen.

Once employees "made the grade," Mildred and Willard were good to work for—the restaurant continues to pay well and offer benefits. Some of their employees, like waitress-turned-cashier Tootie McLear, have been working there for thirty years. "We're like family," she says.

Today, Michael DiGrassie, Mildred's son who now owns and manages the restaurant, is committed to keeping community and employee ties close. The business keeps records of longtime customers' and employees' birthdays and anniversaries and what their favorite menu items are. These folks get cards on those dates, and sometimes more. And

Faithful employee Tootie McLear.

Oyster George, who sells fresh Chesapeake Bay oysters to Mrs. Rowe's Restaurant for Thursday night oyster feasts.

often the restaurant sends meals to those employees and customers who are housebound, in nursing homes, or in personal care facilities. To the men and women who get those cards, cakes, and meals, it means that someone remembers them and appreciates them. Make no mistake, this is Mildred's hand still moving in her family business.

Many women of Mildred's generation never imagined a career outside of the home, let alone running the most successful family-owned restaurant in the state of Virginia. The reasons for Mildred's astounding success are surprisingly simple. The same themes ran continuously through her life—whether as a small girl living on a farm in Rich Patch, or as a young married woman in Covington, or a successful business owner in Staunton—hard work, sacrifice, family, faith, and food.

Her family continues to take an active role in the restaurant. For fifteen years, Mildred's oldest daughter, Brenda Hathaway, helped manage the restaurant. Now, not only does Mildred's son, Michael, manage it, but her grandson Aaron, a schooled chef, is cooking in the kitchen. It seems clear that this is one restaurant that will stay in the family. That would do Mrs. Rowe proud. She was greatly comforted by Aaron's presence in the kitchen. During the last year of her life, sometimes the only way family members could get her to eat was to tell her Aaron cooked it.

A proud Mrs. Rowe with her son Mike and grandson Aaron.

When she passed away at the age of eighty-nine in January 2003, more than six hundred people attended her memorial service—friends, family, employees, local business owners, and state government officials. Recently, her memory was also honored by the state legislature and the Greater Augusta Regional Chamber of Commerce for her contributions to the community. Yet, as one resident put it, "Mildred Rowe had more money than God, but she was always just a girl from Rich Patch."

Chapter 1

Biscuits, Bread & Breakfast Treats

Kicking the Dirt off Corn

*"My mother taught me how to cook. We made a game out of guessing the
ingredients she used for things."*

—Mildred Rowe

Even though the Appalachians were lush with wild berries, herbs, wild
onions, apples, and plenty of good food from the garden, it could be a
harsh place to live. Rich Patch, Virginia, where Mildred was born, is deep
in the hills of the Alleghany Highlands. Today, it has the haunting, ethereal beauty
of a land filled with ancient stories.
Abandoned mines, mills, and old
farmhouses dot the hilly fields and
winding roads. This is a place where
rock and earth meet sky, and nature
almost always has its way.

A small white farmhouse with
no driveway sits off a gravel road
in a hollow down from a curving,
grassy hillside. Cars are parked
along the road. At one time, Ruth
Ann Craft's dahlias framed the
entryway, her roses lined the wire
fence, and her house was filled with
twelve children. One of those children, Mildred, had enough energy
and drive for the whole family. She

*Mildred remembered having sleepovers at her grandmother's
house—known as the Old Rock House.*

won 4-H prizes for her potato crop and didn't have the time or inclination to play
with dolls. Nor did she want to help with cleaning the house, though she did not
mind cleaning the barn and tending the animals.

Born in 1913 to Ruth Ann (Wilson) and James Henry Craft, Mildred was the ninth child in the family. She was the last of the Craft children to be born at her grandmother's house, the Old Rock House, a native limestone I-house, a uniquely American house barn built just after the Civil War.

The year that Mildred was born, five-thousand suffragettes marched in Washington on the day before President Woodrow Wilson's inauguration. It was also the year that Virginia-born Willa Cather published *O Pioneers!* and Mary Johnston released *Hagar*, a feminist manifesto in novel form. Johnston went on to form the Equal Suffrage League, which was headquartered in Three Hills, near Warm Springs, Virginia, very close to Rich Patch. Mildred, of course, was just a baby and was not aware of the political and social wheels already in motion that would pave the way for her accomplishments, even before she took her first step.

> *"Mildred always liked a clean house, but she didn't want to be the one to do it."*
>
> —Virginia Craft Bowers, Mildred's sister

In 2002, the eighty-nine-year-old Mildred visited Rich Patch with her sisters Bertha Mays and Virginia Bowers. Just seeing the house brought memories flooding back for the sisters.

They remembered how their mother gave them saline washes in their noses and mouths during the flu epidemic of 1918. Not one of them got the flu. They remembered how their father became a sawyer for a short time and how it never really worked out for him. They also remembered where all the moonshine stills were hidden.

"There's where so and so had their still," said Mildred, pointing out a patch of woods off the gravel road.

> *"We went to a lot of birthday parties. Sometimes they played the kissing game... the girls would leave the room and I think a boy would call the girl in that he wanted and they'd come in and kiss. I was too young to get in on that."*
>
> —Virginia, Mildred's sister

"We knew where they all where," Virginia said.

"But we never drank any of it," Bertha chimed in.

"Oh no, not us," Mildred said.

The Craft children were brought up Baptist. In those days, that meant no imbibing alcohol or playing cards, which was considered gambling. "One time Mama found a deck of cards in one of my brother's pockets and you'd have thought he'd killed somebody," Virginia says.

Among other things, the boys were in charge of keeping wood chopped for the stove. "My father always thought the girls used way too much wood," remembers John Jr., Mildred's nephew. "He said it seemed like that's all he got done doing."

Coffee sat on the back of their woodstove all day long, oozing a rich, gritty smell that filled the house. The stove had a warming closet that kept food ready and warm for family coming in from the fields.

Mildred Craft, caught on a fence, reaches for her mother.

The Crafts' days were filled with tending the animals—hogs, cows, and chickens—and housekeeping. Their dark hours were lighted by oil lamps, though they usually went to bed at sunset. The kids carried in water from an outside pump that tapped an ice-cold mountain stream. It had to be heated for cleaning and for weekly bathing. The children pitched in with all the chores.

"Mildred'd get up early in morning before anybody else," says ninety-three-year-old Bertha. "By the time the rest of us would get up to go chestnut pickin', she'd have it done."

"We all slept in one big bed together. When one rolled over, we'd all roll over."

—MILDRED ROWE

Mildred loved to pluck things from the earth, trees, and bushes—chestnuts, berries, potatoes, onions—and she also loved to run. One of her early jobs was uncovering the first shoots of corn stalks to give the corn room to grow. She figured out that she could get it done faster if she used her toes instead of bending over and using her hands. A young Mildred on the move, hair flying in the breeze, giggling in the July sun, feet kicking the dirt off corn, forms an apt metaphor for her life—she was always on the move, but with a purpose.

It's easy to see how Mildred's food philosophies were formed in Rich Patch. Like many rural families at the time, the Crafts were subsistence farmers. They had to eat and they ate what they grew, harvested, slaughtered, hunted, fished, and preserved. Cooking was time-consuming, with tasks like peeling potatoes, stirring gravy, and kneading bread dough. The food in Rich Patch informed Mildred's judgment of all food, throughout her whole life. Even with the advent of instant mashed potatoes, canned gravies, and processed vegetables, Mildred never opted for convenience over taste.

> **"I had one doll. Mildred did not like dolls. She had a horse on a stick and that was her favorite toy."**
>
> —VIRGINIA CRAFT BOWERS, MILDRED'S SISTER

It is also easy to see how the lack of food, which farm families often experienced late in winter, and the hunger she felt from time to time, shaped one of her other lifelong philosophies: "If a person is hungry, feed them." And she did so all of her life, especially as a restaurant owner.

Mildred had a lifelong love of animals.

Alabama Biscuits

Nobody knows what makes these biscuits Alabaman. It's an old recipe of Bertha's, a family favorite, and she can't remember where it came from. Michael says eating them hot, slathered with butter, is best. "You might just want to eat the rolls and skip dinner and dessert," he says.

✴ Lightly grease a rimmed baking sheet. Dissolve the yeast in the warm water in a small bowl. Set aside to proof for 5 to 10 minutes, until foamy.

✴ Sift the flour, baking powder, sugar, and salt together into the bowl of a stand mixer or a large bowl. Add the yeast mixture, oil, and milk and mix well. Knead in a stand mixer fitted with the dough hook or by hand for 5 to 7 minutes.

✴ Roll out the dough on a lightly floured surface to a thickness of ¼ inch. Cut out 30 rounds with a 2-inch biscuit cutter. Dip the bottom of 15 of the rounds into the melted butter and stack them on the remaining 15 rounds, to make a total of 15 biscuits. Arrange on the prepared baking sheet and let rise in a warm place away from drafts for 1 hour, until they double in volume.

✴ Preheat the oven to 425°F. Bake the biscuits for about 15 minutes, until nicely browned. Serve at once.

Makes 15 biscuits

1 (¼-ounce) envelope active dry yeast

¼ cup warm water (about 105°F)

2½ cups all-purpose flour

2 teaspoons baking powder

2 tablespoons sugar

½ teaspoon salt

2 tablespoons vegetable oil

¾ cup warm milk (about 105°F)

½ cup unsalted butter, melted

Angel Biscuits

"Disappears" is scribbled near the handwritten recipe in Bertha's old recipe notebook. A light and sweet biscuit that can be cut ahead of time and frozen until you are ready to place in the oven. Letting the dough rounds barely touch during baking yields soft, fluffy sides.

Makes 24 biscuits

* Lightly grease 2 baking sheets. Dissolve the yeast in the warm water in a small bowl. Set aside to proof for 5 to 10 minutes, until foamy and doubled in volume. Stir in the buttermilk.

* Stir together the flour, sugar, baking soda, baking powder, and salt in a large bowl. Cut in the shortening with a pastry blender until the mixture is crumbly. Add the yeast mixture and stir only until the dry ingredients are moist.

* Turn the dough out onto a lightly floured surface and knead 4 or 5 times. Roll the dough out to a thickness of ½ inch. Cut out 24 rounds with a 2-inch biscuit cutter. Arrange the biscuits with their sides barely touching on the prepared baking sheets. Cover with a cloth and let rise in a warm place away from drafts for about 1 hour, until almost doubled in size.

* Preheat the oven to 425°F. Bake the biscuits for 10 to 12 minutes, until golden brown on top. Serve hot.

1 (¼-ounce) envelope active dry yeast

2 tablespoons warm water (about 105°F)

2 cups buttermilk

5 cups all-purpose flour

⅓ cup sugar

1 teaspoon baking soda

3 teaspoons baking powder

2 teaspoons salt

1 cup vegetable shortening

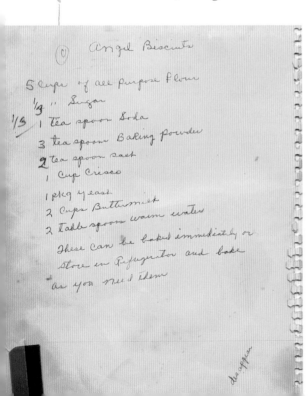

Buttermilk Biscuits

Bertha made these biscuits every day at home when the family lived in Goshen. It's a great mix-and-go recipe, best eaten with apple butter or gravy and fried apples.

✳ Preheat the oven to 425°F. Lightly grease a baking sheet.

✳ Stir together the flour, salt, sugar, and baking powder in a bowl. Cut in the shortening with a pastry blender until the mixture is crumbly. Stir in the buttermilk to form a soft dough. Do not overmix because too much handling makes the biscuits tough.

✳ Roll out the dough on a lightly floured surface to a thickness of ½ inch. Cut out 15 rounds with a 2-inch biscuit cutter and place them on the prepared baking sheet.

✳ Bake the biscuits for about 15 minutes, until browned. Serve immediately.

Makes 15 biscuits

2 cups all-purpose flour

1 teaspoon salt

1 tablespoon sugar

4 teaspoons baking powder

⅔ cup vegetable shortening

1 cup buttermilk

Hot Rolls

These rolls are especially good for sopping up gravy left on your plate after dinner—which makes cleaning a little easier.

✳ Lightly grease two 9 by 9-inch baking dishes. Dissolve the yeast in the warm water in a small bowl. Set aside to proof for 5 to 10 minutes, until foamy and nearly doubled in volume.

✳ Stir together the boiling water and butter in a large bowl. Stir in the sugar and salt, then the milk, and then the yeast mixture. Stir in enough flour to make a soft dough. Transfer to a well-greased bowl, turning to grease the top of the dough. Cover and let rise in a warm place away from drafts for 15 minutes, until it doubles in volume.

✳ Preheat the oven to 400°F. Punch down the dough. With greased fingers, pinch off golf ball–size pieces of dough and roll into 24 smooth round rolls. Arrange the rolls in the prepared baking dishes 1½ inches apart. Cover and let rise in a warm place away from drafts for 15 minutes, until they double in volume.

✳ Bake the rolls for about 15 minutes, until golden. Serve hot.

Makes 24 rolls

2 (¼-ounce) envelopes active dry yeast, or 2 yeast cakes

¼ cup warm water (about 105°F)

¾ cup boiling water

4 tablespoons unsalted butter, melted

3 tablespoons sugar

2 teaspoons salt

1 cup milk

5½ to 6 cups all-purpose flour

Orange Blossoms

These muffins were a Christmas family favorite. In Goshen, Mildred and her sisters and children would bake gingerbread, orange blossoms, and coconut cake. The smell of the baking, mixed with the scent of pine and popcorn, filled the air. Some folks would be stringing popcorn; others would be making pine garlands. The children collected Virginia creeper and wild holly for decorating. Mildred's daughter Ginger's favorite Christmas treat were the orange blossoms. She says, "I have tried to make them, but they are just not as good as Mom's." These muffins are little orange puffs of flavor.

✳ Preheat the oven to 350°F. Butter the cups of a 1-ounce muffin tin or line with paper cups.

✳ Sift the flour, baking powder, and salt together into a bowl. In a separate large bowl, combine the eggs, water, vanilla, and granulated sugar and mix well. Add the flour mixture to the egg mixture and mix well. Fill the muffin cups three-quarters full of batter.

✳ Bake the muffins for 10 minutes, until browned. Stir together the orange juice and zest, lemon juice and zest, and confectioners' sugar in a bowl. Remove the muffins from the tin and while still warm, dip the tops into the sugar mixture. Place the muffins on aluminum foil or waxed paper to cool. Serve at room temperature.

Makes 24 miniature muffins

1½ cups all-purpose flour

1½ teaspoons baking powder

½ teaspoon salt

3 eggs, lightly beaten

½ cup water

1 teaspoon pure vanilla extract

1⅓ cups granulated sugar

Juice of 2 oranges

Grated zest of 2 oranges

Juice of 2 lemons

Grated zest of 2 lemons

4 cups confectioners' sugar

Banana-Nut Bread

For those who don't like them, raisins can be left out of this recipe and it's still delicious. Try grilling the bread in a hot skillet, buttered and browned on both sides.

✳ Preheat the oven to 350°F. Butter and flour a 9 by 5 by 3-inch loaf pan.

✳ Stir together the flour and baking soda in a bowl. In a separate large bowl, beat together the butter and sugar with an electric mixer. One at a time, add the eggs, beating well after each addition. Gradually mix in the flour mixture. Dust the pecans and raisins with flour and stir into the batter. Stir in the mashed bananas. Scrape the batter into the prepared loaf pan.

✳ Bake for about 50 minutes, until a tester inserted into the center comes out clean. Transfer to a wire rack and allow to cool in the pan for 10 minutes. Turn the loaf out of the pan and allow to cool completely. Wrap the loaf in aluminum foil and let sit at room temperature for 1 to 2 days before serving. This allows the bread to become more moist. Serve at room temperature.

Makes 1 loaf

1½ cups all-purpose flour

¾ teaspoon baking soda

½ cup unsalted butter, at room temperature

1 cup sugar

2 eggs

½ cup chopped pecans

½ cup raisins

3 ripe bananas, mashed

Cherry Bread

Substitute dried sour cherries for a real treat in this recipe.

✳   Preheat the oven to 350°F. Lightly grease or spray a 9 by 5 by 3-inch glass or light metal loaf pan. (If using a dark metal pan, decrease the baking temperature to 325°F.)

✳   Stir together the flour, salt, and baking powder in a bowl. In a separate large bowl, beat together the sugar and eggs using with an electric mixer until light and frothy. Alternately add the flour mixture and the reserved cherry juice to the egg mixture, beginning and ending with the dry ingredients. Dust the cherries and pecans with flour and stir into the batter. Scrape the batter into the prepared loaf pan.

✳   Bake for 50 to 60 minutes, until a tester inserted into the center comes out clean. Transfer to a wire rack and allow to cool in the pan for 10 minutes. Turn the loaf out of the pan and allow to cool completely. Serve at room temperature.

Makes 1 loaf

1½ cups all-purpose flour

1 teaspoon salt

1½ teaspoons baking powder

1 cup sugar

2 eggs

1 (6-ounce) jar maraschino cherries, drained with juice reserved, halved

¾ cup chopped pecans

Skillet Cornbread

One of Mildred's favorite snacks was called "soakers"—fresh cornbread crumbled into a tall glass of milk or buttermilk. She ate it with a big spoon while sitting in her favorite chair and watching television. She made skillet cornbread almost every day. Virginia's version of the recipe calls for ¼ cup less cornmeal, which yields a flakier, less crumbly cornbread.

❋ Preheat the oven to 450°F. Place the butter in a 10-inch cast-iron skillet and place in the oven to heat.

❋ Sift the cornmeal, flour, sugar, salt, and baking powder together into a large bowl. Add the eggs and milk and mix well. Remove the hot skillet from the oven, pour the melted butter into the batter and mix well. Scrape the batter into the skillet and bake for about 15 minutes, until golden brown. Serve hot.

Makes one 10-inch cake

2 tablespoons unsalted butter

¾ cup cornmeal

1 cup all-purpose flour

2 tablespoons sugar

½ teaspoon salt

3 teaspoons baking powder

2 eggs, well beaten

⅔ cup milk

Willard's Cornbread

Before he ever met Mildred, Willard had fashioned his own cornbread. His recipe makes two cakes, rather than just one like Mildred's.

❋ Preheat the oven to 425°F. Butter two 8-inch skillets.

❋ Sift the cornmeal, flour, sugar, and baking powder together into a large bowl. Stir in the milk and egg. Stir in the shortening. Scrape the batter into the prepared pans and bake for about 30 minutes, until browned. Cut each cake into 4 wedges and serve hot.

Makes two 8-inch cakes

¾ cup cornmeal

1 cup all-purpose flour

¼ cup sugar

3 teaspoons baking powder

1 cup milk

1 egg, well beaten

3 tablespoons vegetable shortening, unsalted butter, or lard, melted

Spoon Bread

A cross between a cornmeal soufflé and polenta, spoon bread fills your mouth with a subtle, sweet puff of corn. It was added to the menu at Rowe's in the early 1990s. From time to time, Mildred had taken her children to eat at a cafeteria in Roanoke and they had loved the spoon bread there. Later on, as adults working in the restaurant, they wanted to add it to the menu. After a few fits and starts, Barbara Marshall, a cook at Rowe's, volunteered a recipe she knew of from previous work. They tried it, and with a couple of changes, the spoon bread has become a big hit with customers. Here is the version that is being served today.

✳ Preheat the oven to 350°F. Butter a 9 by 13-inch baking dish.

✳ Heat the milk and butter in a large saucepan over medium-high heat. When the milk begins to steam, add the cornmeal and cook, whisking constantly, for 2 minutes, until smooth. Remove from the heat and let cool and thicken slightly.

✳ Whisk the eggs, sugar, baking powder, and salt together in a bowl. Add the egg mixture to the cooled cornmeal mixture and mix well. Scrape the batter into the prepared baking dish and bake for 30 to 40 minutes, until golden brown. Serve hot with butter. (The batter can be refrigerated for up to 6 hours before baking, but increase the baking time by 10 minutes. Spoon bread reheats well in the microwave, although it will dry out a bit.)

Serves 10

4 cups milk

½ cup unsalted butter

1 cup cornmeal

4 eggs, lightly beaten

6 teaspoons sugar

1 tablespoon baking powder

¾ teaspoon salt

Spoon Bread Soufflé

Bertha added a unique twist to the spoon bread experiment with this more delicate recipe.

✳ Preheat the oven to 350°F. Butter a 9-inch deep baking dish.

✳ Heat the milk in a large saucepan over medium-high heat. When the milk begins to steam, add the cornmeal and cook, whisking constantly, for 2 minutes, until smooth. Remove from the heat and let cool and thicken slightly.

✳ Whisk the egg yolks, salt, sugar, butter, and baking powder together in a large bowl. Add the egg yolk mixture to the cornmeal mixture and mix well. Using an electric mixer, beat the whites in a bowl until stiff peaks form. Fold the egg whites into the cornmeal mixture.

✳ Scrape the batter into the prepared baking dish and bake for about 45 minutes, until golden brown. Serve immediately.

Serves 6

3 cups milk

¾ cup cornmeal

5 eggs, separated

1½ teaspoons salt

3 tablespoons sugar

5 tablespoons unsalted butter, melted

1½ teaspoon baking powder

Pumpkin-Pecan Pancakes

This recipe was featured in Southern Living *magazine as one of the South's most unique restaurant breakfasts. It is a rich and hearty dish, with warm, comforting spices that help greet the day.*

✻ Sift the flour, baking powder, cinnamon, nutmeg, allspice, and sugar together into a large bowl. In a separate large bowl, combine the pumpkin, eggs, milk, oil, and vanilla. Add the flour mixture to the pumpkin mixture and mix well. Fold in the pecans.

✻ Heat a greased griddle over medium-high heat. Using ¼ cup of batter for each pancake, spoon the batter onto the griddle. Cook the pancakes on the first side until bubbles form in the center and they are browned on the bottom. Turn and brown the other side. Serve hot with warmed maple syrup.

Serves 4

2 cups all-purpose flour

4 teaspoons baking powder

1 teaspoon ground cinnamon

½ teaspoon ground nutmeg

¼ teaspoon ground allspice

¾ cup sugar

1½ cups pumpkin purée

3 eggs

1 cup milk

¾ cup vegetable oil

1 teaspoon pure vanilla extract

½ cup chopped pecans

Maple syrup, for serving

Rowe's Regular Pancakes

The story goes that Mildred's mother often made buttermilk buckwheat pancakes. She'd mix up the batter at night and leave the pot beside the woodstove all night long. Unfortunately, after much searching, we have not been able to find this recipe and we're not sure that one ever existed. In the meantime, Rowe's regular pancakes are tried and true, and kids love them, especially if you throw in a handful of chocolate chips.

Makes 12 to 16 pancakes

1¾ cups all-purpose flour

4 teaspoons sugar

3 teaspoons baking powder

½ teaspoon salt

1½ cups milk

2 eggs, lightly beaten

2 tablespoons vegetable oil

✳ Sift the flour, sugar, baking powder, and salt together into a large bowl. Add the milk and eggs and mix with an electric mixer on low speed until well blended and smooth. Mix in the oil. (Batter can be kept in a tightly covered container and kept for up to 1 week.)

✳ Heat a greased griddle over medium-high heat. Using ¼ cup of batter for each pancake, spoon the batter onto the griddle. Cook the pancakes on the first side until bubbles form in the center and they are browned on the bottom. Turn and brown the other side. Serve hot with warm maple syrup.

Milk Toast

During the last year of his life, sometimes all that Willard could eat was comforting, mellow, milk toast.

Serves 4 to 6

2 cups milk

1 teaspoon salt

1 teaspoon sugar

6 slices hot, buttered toast

✳ Combine the milk, salt, and sugar in a saucepan and bring to a boil over high heat. Arrange the toast on plates and pour the hot milk mixture over. Serve immediately.

French Toast

The vanilla added to this classic dish gives it an extra richness. Use cinnamon-raisin bread for even more flavor.

✳ Whisk the eggs, milk, sugar, cinnamon, and vanilla together in a shallow container.

✳ Melt the butter in a large skillet or on a griddle over medium-high heat. One at a time, thoroughly coat the bread slices on both sides in the egg mixture. Remove the bread from the batter, letting any excess drip off. Fry the toast until golden brown and crispy on both sides. Serve hot with butter and syrup.

Serves 4 to 6

4 eggs, lightly beaten

1 cup milk

2 teaspoons sugar

2 teaspoons ground cinnamon

½ teaspoon pure vanilla extract

8 (1-inch-thick) slices day-old homemade bread

2 tablespoons unsalted butter, plus more for serving

Maple syrup, for serving

Creamed Eggs on Toast

"This was a real treat, especially for breakfast," says Brenda Hathaway, Mildred's daughter. For a brunch or lunch variation, slice the egg whites and crumble the egg yolks. Then garnish the top with parsley sprigs.

✳ Peel and slice the eggs. Place the toast on plates and arrange the egg slices over the toast. Pour the sauce over the eggs and toast and serve at once.

Serves 4 to 6

8 hard-boiled eggs

8 slices hot, buttered toast

1 cup Medium White Sauce, warmed (page 32)

Chapter 2

Sauces, Gravies & Preserves

You Can Take the Girl Out of the Farm . . .

"Lard is a gift from God."

—MILDRED ROWE

Mildred, Bertha, and, soon, Virginia straddled two worlds during the Depression. They lived in the quiet mountains and drove every day to the bustling factory town of Covington to work in the International Rayon Factory, with the whirring, rhythmic sounds of huge machines and the smell of silk in the air, a far cry from their quiet mountain farm. Mildred soon became a supervisor and then moved on to work in grocery and department stores.

The Craft family had lost their farm in the uncertain economic climate and moved to a rented farmhouse nearby. They still farmed, but life would never be the same. Covington was the closest town of any size to Rich Patch, and it took some time to reach in their Model T Ford. But it was natural for the girls to look for work there, even though it departed from the traditional path for the daughters of farmers in the region.

Mildred and Bertha bought the Model T together. Mildred enjoyed driving and always wanted to be the one to do it. Bertha told Mildred to either let her drive more or to give her share of the money back. Bertha wanted to purchase a wrap-around front porch for her mother. Mildred came up with the money and began her love affair with the road.

Mildred loved to drive fast. She also liked to sightsee while driving and so often veered off the

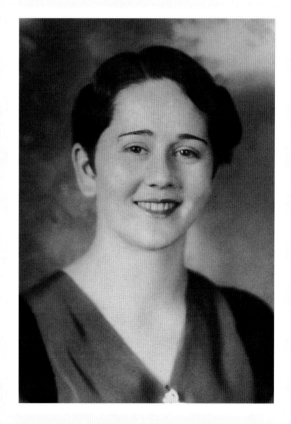

An eighteen-year-old Mildred Craft.

road. Shortly after she moved to Staunton later in life, she was stopped for speeding with only her Sunday purse, which did not contain her license. This was the first of many speeding tickets she would get from the Staunton police. She received her last speeding ticket when she was eighty-five years old.

"Do you know who I am?" she asked the young police officer, perhaps hoping he'd come by the restaurant for some pie rather than give her a ticket. "Yes, Ma'am, I do," he replied. "And you are still getting a ticket."

The Depression formed Mildred's sense of economy. Like so many people who struggled during this time, she was forced to be creative and thrifty with what she had. She also developed a sense of proportion. She knew how to portion food, and how to stretch it, if need be.

A bone-deep appreciation of farm fresh food was not the only thing Mildred took away from Rich Patch. She believed in using every part of every edible thing that grew from the earth, had wings, or walked on four legs. Today, her restaurant

Mildred and Virginia pause for a quick pose before going off to work, perhaps at the International Rayon Factory.

Career girls: Mildred, Bertha, and Pearl Craft at the home place.

About Covington

Covington, where the DiGrassies lived and worked for thirteen years, is a working-class town. It had several factories and a lively downtown area, with shops and other conveniences. Today, the paper giant MeadWestvaco is the town company.

By the time Mildred and her sisters lived in Covington, the town had almost two hundred years of history. In 1746, Peter Wright came from New York to become the first settler on a parcel of 286 acres that was to become the site of Covington. The town grew into a hotbed of industry around the turn of the nineteenth century.

---

is one of the few places that features breakfast scrapple (*pon haus*), a mysterious mixture of pork innards rolled in spices and then fried. It's a delicacy found mostly in the Appalachians, especially those parts settled by the Pennsylvania Germans in the 1700s and early 1800s.

Mildred's breed of Southern cooking was country, pure and simple. Folks in the Virginia Highlands did not eat shrimp or oysters, though some ate river eels. In the subsistence tradition of the Appalachians, they ate what was close to them. During the hunting season, they may have had the treat of venison. When the living was good, they ate pork, beef, and plenty of chicken. Fatty, rich gravy was a mainstay, and just one way to stretch valuable meat stock.

As Mildred and her sisters explored Covington, they saw and experienced things they never imagined: grocery stores filled with ready-made food, sit-down restaurants where waitresses brought food that someone else had cooked. The shops, factories, and restaurants had electricity, something the Craft sisters were unaccustomed to. And they didn't wear

Mildred and her prized possession.

About the Homestead

The Homestead is an elegant, world-renowned resort built around mineral springs in around 1750. Homesteaders built simple wooden guest cabins near the best springs and visitors wrote about their medicinal properties. George Washington visited in 1755 and 1756.

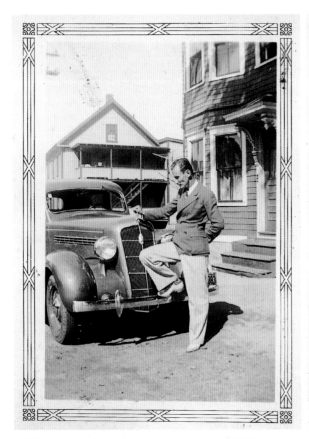

Mildred called the dapper Eugene her "Grassi." That was allegedly his original last name. He changed it to DiGrassi when he moved to Covington and started his new life. Other family members later changed the spelling of the family name to DiGrassie.

The menus at her successful Staunton restaurant bear this photograph of Mildred, which was taken by Eugene in New Hampshire. The family chose this picture because it captures her spirit.

A handmade Valentine from Eugene to Mildred.

Eugene and Mildred were married for six years without conceiving a baby. A disillusioned Mildred finally went to the mountain women she knew growing up. They told her to drink mare's serum. It did the trick. Their first daughter, Brenda, was often told she was a "mare's serum baby."

The young DiGrassie family.

Mildred with her daughters Brenda and Linda celebrating Christmas in Covington.

their simple, cotton farm dresses anymore, but dressed the part of working girls. They shopped for clothes, hose, handbags, and shoes—one of Mildred's lifelong passions. In their daily travels, they also met a wider variety of men than they ever did on their mountain farm. One such man was Eugene DiGrassie, who, when he first saw the beautiful, vivacious Mildred Craft, predicted to his coworker that he would marry her, and he did.

Mildred and Eugene were madly in love, but very different people. Married in May 1934, in the middle of the Depression, Mildred had probably never met anybody like the educated, sophisticated Eugene DiGrassie. He was French-Italian, Catholic, and Yankee. All rare, even in the industrial town of Covington. He was more concerned with his grooming, clothing, and posture than the men she knew in Rich Patch, who we were mostly farmers, miners, and factory workers.

When Mildred met him, Eugene was designing window displays and selling shoes at Rooklin's department store in the downtown area. By that time, Mildred was a bookkeeper at Foster's department store and was learning about business. But Eugene dreamed of owning his own business and of living the good life. He did not plan on being in retail forever. He liked to talk about his ideas; maybe that is what lit the fire between them because Mildred had ideas too.

> *When going out to eat at a new restaurant, Mildred would often check out the bathroom first. "If the bathrooms are clean, the kitchens are clean," she said.*

When they first married, the young couple moved to Eugene's home state of New Hampshire. There, Mildred not only felt left out because the family spoke

An unusually elegant Mildred DiGrassie dining at the Homestead in the early 1940s.

French, but also because she missed the "real food" of home. So, they moved back to Covington and joined Mildred's sisters and their husbands in one big house on Fudge Street. As often as they could, Mildred and Eugene would steal away to dine at the Homestead resort, surrounding themselves with the elegance of French food, wine, and a live orchestra.

In the late thirties and early forties, when Mildred and Eugene dined there, it had three different restaurants, all grand affairs. These restaurants were modeled after the big New York (mostly French) restaurants.

Coming from a different, more cosmopolitan, background, Eugene knew French food, which was so different from the down home country cooking that Mildred knew and loved. Mildred's love of Southern food was so ingrained in her personality that it could not to be ignored.

Eugene's mother was French; Saint Germaine was her maiden name. His maternal aunt owned a French restaurant in Montreal and his brother owned a restaurant in Plattsburgh, New York. Fine food and the restaurant business were in Eugene's background. One dish we know Eugene taught Mildred to make was spaghetti, which was exotic in the 1930s. Italian food was a new arrival in places like Covington.

Even though Mildred's first food love was mountain, country cooking, and she never ventured into French cooking, she learned Italian cooking from Eugene, who

was a willing teacher in the kitchen with her. She understood the Italian side of his heritage, at least when it came to food. Her restaurant still offers a less spicy version of his spaghetti recipe.

Imagine a typical 1930s kitchen—a gas stove; a sink, probably stained by the local sulfuric water; and maybe an icebox. Eugene standing beside Mildred at the hot stove, the lush aroma of oregano, marjoram, garlic, olive oil, and tomatoes frothing together. She probably had never had spaghetti before. Even if she had tried the canned version on the market, it could not have been as good as the real thing. Tasting spaghetti sauce for the first time must have awakened slumbering taste buds.

SAUCES

Some folks go to their graves without divulging their special sauce recipes. When *Mrs. Rowe's Favorite Recipes* came out, her barbecue sauce recipe was not included anywhere. In fact, the recipes in that book call for jars of Mrs. Rowe's Short Rib Sauce or Pork Barbecue Sauce. The family decided to be more forthcoming in this book.

Cocktail Sauce

For a smokier variation on this popular sauce, add 1 tablespoon Worcestershire sauce and 1 tablespoon freshly squeezed lemon juice.

✶ Combine all of the ingredients in a small bowl and mix until well combined. Store covered and refrigerated for up to 1 week.

Makes about 2 cups

1¾ cups ketchup

1 to 2 tablespoons prepared horseradish

1 tablespoon hot sauce

Tartar Sauce

Slather this on your favorite fish or dip your French fries in it as an alternative to ketchup.

✶ Combine all of the ingredients in a small bowl and mix until well combined. The sauce can be covered and refrigerated for up to 1 week.

Makes about 2 cups

1½ cups creamy salad dressing

½ cup pickle relish

1 tablespoon hot sauce

DiGrassie's Spaghetti Sauce

This is the real thing, DiGrassie's original recipe—a variation of what is served at the restaurant but an important family recipe all the same.

✳ Heat the oil over medium-high heat in a large, heavy pot. Add the onion and cook, stirring frequently, for about 5 minutes, until it begins to soften. Add the ground chuck and cook, stirring often, for about 10 minutes, until the meat is crumbled and thoroughly browned. Stir in the garlic, mushrooms, parsley, tomato sauce, diced tomatoes, tomato paste, salt, pepper, sugar, and basil. Decrease the heat to medium-low, cover the pot, and simmer for 1 hour. Stir in the wine, replace the cover, and simmer for 1 more hour.

✳ Serve at once or cool and cover. Refrigerate for up to 1 week or freeze to up to 1 year. This sauce freezes well.

Makes about 2 quarts

¼ cup olive oil

1 small onion, minced

1 pound ground chuck

2 cloves garlic, minced

2 (4-ounce) cans sliced mushrooms, undrained

¼ cup finely chopped fresh parsley

1 (8-ounce) can tomato sauce

1 (14.5-ounce) can diced tomatoes

1 (6-ounce) can tomato paste

1 teaspoon salt

½ teaspoon freshly ground black pepper

¼ teaspoon sugar

1 teaspoon dried basil

1 cup red wine

*"**My sister Linda had a spaghetti sauce radar. Somehow, she knew when the sauce was on the stove and would stop by Mother's house just in time to get a quart of sauce for her supper.**"*

—MICHAEL DIGRASSIE, MILDRED'S SON

Pork Barbecue Sauce

When Willard Rowe first purchased Perk's Barbecue (the restaurant's original name) in 1947, he was not fond of the sauce. He and his mother traveled to North Carolina seeking the best sauce they could find. They purchased this recipe for $100. This is the first time that it has been published.

✳ Heat the oil in a large saucepan over medium-high heat. Add the onions and cook, stirring frequently, for about 10 minutes, until softened. Add the remaining ingredients and stir to mix well. Increase the heat to high and bring to a boil. Decrease the heat to medium-low and simmer uncovered, stirring occasionally, for 15 to 20 minutes, until the sauce thickens slightly. Allow to cool, then cover and refrigerate for up to 2 weeks.

Makes about 2 cups

1 tablespoon oil

2 onions, finely chopped

1 teaspoon dried parsley flakes

1 teaspoon dried thyme

1 cup ketchup

1½ cups tomato juice

½ cup sugar

¼ cup yellow mustard

1½ tablespoons prepared horseradish

1 teaspoon chili powder

½ teaspoon paprika

1 tablespoon pickle relish

Got Sauce?

Brenda Hathaway, Mildred's oldest daughter, writes in *Mrs. Rowe's Favorite Recipes*: "Mother used to make a huge pot of spaghetti sauce and supply our entire family (actually five families) with a source for a delicious quick meal. We usually called and said 'Hey Mom, got any spaghetti sauce?' Her reply was either 'Come on over, I'll get it out of the freezer' or 'No, but give me a couple of hours, and I'll have you some.'"

Short Rib Sauce

This is an extremely versatile sauce that, according to Michael, can be used on beef ribs, minced beef barbecue, chicken, and meatballs. This is the first time the recipe has been published. Many customers at Rowe's are loyal barbecue fans. Betsy Fultz, and so many like her, comes in just for the barbecue. "I order it every time," she says. "It's so tender, it just about melts in your mouth."

✳ Stir all of the ingredients together in a saucepan and bring to a boil over high heat. Decrease the heat to medium-low and simmer uncovered, stirring occasionally, for 15 to 20 minutes, until the sauce thickens. Allow to cool, then cover and refrigerate for up to 2 weeks.

Makes about 4 cups

2 cups ketchup

½ cup freshly squeezed lemon juice

¼ cup Worcestershire sauce

1 tablespoon yellow mustard

1 cup sugar

1 tablespoon salt

2 tablespoons minced onion

Karl Craig, one of the finest cooks in Virginia.

Sweet and Sour Sauce

The perfect sauce for chicken, stir-fried vegetables, or whatever you want to spice up with a tangy sweet and sour flavor. This is just the kind of sauce that Mildred loved to play her ingredient game with: "What do you think is in it?" she'd say. If someone asked her the same question about a sauce she'd never had before, her tasting ability was so exceptional that she would often know exactly what the ingredients were. In addition, she'd often give an opinion on what was lacking.

✳ Combine the vinegar, sugar, 1½ cups of the water, salt, bell pepper, and pimientos in a large saucepan over medium-high heat. Bring to a boil and stir until the sugar dissolves. Let the mixture boil, stirring occasionally, for 15 minutes.

✳ Stir the cornstarch and the remaining ¼ cup water together in a small bowl to make a smooth slurry. Pour the slurry into the boiling sauce and stir for about 2 minutes, until the sauce thickens. Remove the pot from the heat and stir in the paprika. Allow to cool, then cover and refrigerate for up to 1 week.

Makes about 4 cups

1½ cups apple cider vinegar

3½ cups sugar

1¾ cups water

Pinch of salt

½ green bell pepper, finely chopped

2 tablespoons diced pimientos

3 tablespoons cornstarch

3 teaspoons paprika

BASIC WHITE SAUCES

White sauces in various degrees of thickness are used in many Rowe recipes. Very little changes from one ingredient list to the next, but it's always important to use the proper version when a recipe calls for one.

Thin White Sauce

Best for salmon cakes and chicken-fried steak.

✳ Melt the butter in a saucepan over low heat. Whisk in the flour, salt, and pepper, stirring until smooth. Gradually whisk in the milk. Increase the heat to medium-high and cook, whisking constantly, until bubbling and thick enough to coat the back of a spoon, about 8 to 10 minutes. Use immediately.

Makes about 1½ cups

1 tablespoon unsalted butter

1 tablespoon all-purpose flour

¼ teaspoon salt

Pinch of freshly ground white pepper

1½ cups milk

Medium White Sauce

Used for breakfast gravies.

✳ Melt the butter in a saucepan over low heat. Whisk in the flour, salt, and pepper, stirring until smooth. Gradually whisk in the milk. Increase the heat to medium-high and cook, whisking constantly, until bubbling and thick enough to coat the back of a spoon, about 8 to 10 minutes. Use immediately.

Makes about 1 cup

2 tablespoons unsalted butter

2 tablespoons all-purpose flour

¼ teaspoon salt

Pinch of freshly ground white pepper

1 cup milk

Thick White Sauce

More appropriate for baked dishes, like country-style steak.

✳ Melt the butter in a saucepan over low heat. Whisk in the flour, salt, and pepper, stirring until smooth. Gradually whisk in the milk. Increase the heat to medium-high and cook, whisking constantly, until bubbling and thick enough to coat the back of a spoon, about 8 to 10 minutes. Use immediately.

Makes about 1 cup

3 tablespoons unsalted butter

¼ cup all-purpose flour

¼ teaspoon salt

Pinch of freshly ground white pepper

1 cup milk

"*Don't forget that I saw you going down the old road Monday leading a mule singing 'Me and My Shadow.' Mildred told me that your cow would not give milk so you sold HIM. Baloney!*"

—Earl [Mildred and Bertha's brother, in Bertha's autograph book]

GRAVIES

Aaron DiGrassie, on gravy: "Americans tend to view gravy as a Southern tradition. But when I think about my grandmother and gravy, what's interesting is that while she was growing up in the hills of Rich Patch making gravy, there were other children learning those same techniques in places like France and Italy. Of course, there was a little variation here and there, which depended on what kind of ingredients were on hand and how much time they had to experiment."

Sausage Gravy

"Rowe's has the best sausage gravy I have ever tasted," local customer Beverly Brown says. She, like many of the locals, has been frequenting the restaurant for forty-some years.

✱   Place a large, heavy skillet over medium heat. Add the sausage and cook for 5 to 10 minutes, until cooked through and no longer pink. Using a slotted spoon, transfer the sausage to a plate lined with paper towels to drain.

✱   Pour all but 4 tablespoons of the drippings out of the skillet, leaving any browned bits on the bottom. Place the skillet over medium heat and scrape up the browned bits with a spatula. Whisk in the flour, salt, and pepper and cook, whisking constantly, for 10 minutes, until the mixture is browned and smooth. Remove the skillet from the heat and gradually stir in the milk and water. Return the skillet to medium-high heat and cook, whisking constantly, until bubbling and thick enough to coat the back of a spoon, about 8 to 10 minutes.

✱   Stir the sausage into the gravy and season to taste with salt and pepper. Serve at once or keep warm over low heat. Store covered and refrigerated for up to 1 week.

Makes about 6 cups

1 pound crumbled sausage patties or bulk sausage

¾ cup all-purpose flour

1 teaspoon salt

Pinch of freshly ground white pepper

1½ cups milk

1½ cups water

Salt and freshly ground black pepper

One of the things Michael remembers most about living in Goshen was that they had gravy at every meal— breakfast, lunch, and supper.

Pot Gravy

Makin' that beef stock stretch, in the Appalachian tradition.

✳   Bring the broth to a boil in a large pot over high heat. Stir the flour and water together in a small bowl to make a smooth paste. Remove the broth from the heat and slowly stir in the flour mixture. Return the pot to medium heat and cook, whisking constantly, until the gravy thickens to the desired consistency. For table gravy, cook for 7 to 10 minutes to keep it thick. For gravy for baking, cook for 3 to 5 minutes to keep it thin; it will thicken in the oven. Stir in the salt and pepper. Serve at once or keep warm over low heat. Store covered and refrigerated for up to 1 week.

Makes about 4 cups

4 cups beef broth

3 tablespoons all-purpose flour

½ cup water

1 teaspoon salt

½ teaspoon freshly ground black pepper

Chipped Beef Gravy

Mildred made a point of personally teaching Aaron how to make her chipped beef gravy so the tradition would not be lost. He still does it her way, every day.

✳   Melt the butter in a saucepan over low heat. Whisk in the flour, salt, and pepper and stir until smooth. Gradually whisk in the milk and cook, stirring constantly, for 10 minutes, until the mixture begins to thicken. Stir in the dried beef and continue cooking, stirring constantly, until bubbling and thick enough to coat the back of a spoon, about 8 to 10 minutes. Serve at once or keep warm over low heat. Store covered and refrigerated for up to 1 week.

Makes 4 to 6 cups

4 tablespoons unsalted butter

¼ cup all-purpose flour

½ teaspoon salt

Pinch of freshly ground white pepper

2 cups milk

2 (6-ounce) packages dried beef, chopped

PRESERVES

Mrs. Rowe's preserves are famous. You can buy them at the restaurant or from www.mrsrowes.com. When Mildred was in the middle of a batch of preserves, she wouldn't stop until everything was prepared. Once, she was preserving in the restaurant kitchen. Michael came in to tell her that the governor of Virginia was there and would like to meet her. She waved him away. "I can't stop what I'm doing now, especially not for some damned politician."

Preserves are not just for bread. Use them as filling for turnovers, doughnuts, cakes, and jelly rolls. When they are cooking, perserves reach jelling point when the liquid holds together as it drops off a spoon.

Strawberry Preserves

Mildred liked to take her grandchildren to pick strawberries. After the berries had been in the warm car and gotten real juicy, she'd place a container of them on her front porch and tell the kids that it was theirs. The kids would sit on the porch eating the sun-ripened berries while Mildred began making her preserves inside.

Makes about 2 quarts

8 cups crushed strawberries

8 cups (4 pounds) sugar

⅓ cup freshly squeezed lemon juice

✳ Alternate layers of strawberries and sugar in a large, heavy pot. Let stand in a cool place for 5 hours.

✳ Place the pot over medium-high heat and slowly bring to a boil, stirring occasionally until the sugar dissolves. Boil rapidly for about 20 minutes, until it reaches the jelling point. As the preserves thicken, stir frequently to prevent sticking. Stir in the lemon juice and boil for 2 minutes longer. Remove the pot from the heat and skim off any foam.

✳ Ladle the hot preserves into hot, sterilized canning jars, leaving ¼ inch of headspace. Seal immediately following the canning instructions on page 61.

Cherry Preserves

* Stir the cherries and water together in a large, heavy pot. Bring to a boil over medium-high heat and cook, stirring occasionally, for 20 minutes. Gradually stir in the sugar. Continue cooking to the jelling point, about 25 minutes. As the preserves begin to thicken, stir constantly to prevent sticking. Remove the pot from the heat and skim off any foam. Stir in the food coloring.

* Ladle the hot preserves into hot, sterilized canning jars, leaving ¼ inch of headspace. Seal immediately following the canning instructions on page 61.

Makes about 3 pints

3 pounds pitted red cherries

1 cup water

6 cups (3 pounds) sugar

3 to 4 drops red food coloring

*"**Love is pretty, love is handsome**

Love is pretty while it is new

But as love grows older

Love grows colder

And it passeth away

Like the morning dew."*

—Mother [written by Ruth Ann in Bertha's autograph book], July 21, 1928

Raspberry or Blackberry Jam

* Stir the berries and sugar together in a large, heavy pot. Place the pot over medium-high heat and slowly bring to a boil, stirring until the sugar dissolves. Boil rapidly for about 20 minutes, until it reaches the jelling point. As the jam thickens, stir frequently to prevent sticking. Stir in the lemon juice and boil for 2 minutes longer. Remove the pot from the heat and skim off any foam.

* Ladle the hot preserves into hot, sterilized canning jars, leaving ¼ inch of headspace. Seal immediately following the canning instructions on page 61.

Makes about 3 pints

9 cups crushed raspberries or blackberries

6 cups (3 pounds) sugar

¼ cup freshly squeezed lemon juice

Chapter 3

Salads, Dressings & Relishes

When One Door Closes . . .

"Land O'Goshen!"

—Mildred Rowe

As the Paxton family settled down one evening in 1946, a knock was heard on their door. When John Paxton, director of the Millboro Bank, opened it, he saw four wide-eyed people standing there—Bertha and Basil Mays, and Eugene and Mildred DiGrassie. They came to speak to him at home, which was out of the ordinary realm of things, to be sure, but he was impressed with their excitement and verve.

Mildred and her sister and their husbands wanted to purchase the gas station and restaurant in the village of Goshen. The four of them didn't own a thing and had no money. It probably went against Paxton's judgment, but he loaned them the money anyway. He couldn't shake the feeling that there was something about Mildred. She had a spark, and he knew that if she was anything like she seemed, the restaurant would be a success.

By that time, Mildred knew that her marriage to Eugene was over, even though he stood beside her, perhaps with his arm around her waist. But she was sure that the restaurant plan would work. As long as he stayed behind in

A fifteen-year-old Carroll Mays helping at the gas station.

Covington, and as long as she had her children and a way to make a living, she did not care what he did. By this time, she was sick of people talking behind her back and wondering what was going on between Eugene and another woman.

A view of the station, which was around the corner from the eatery.

"You won't find any pictures of Mildred when she lived here, she never stood still long enough."

—Goshen resident

The Goshen home.

"I am not sure what the amount of the loan was, but I know they paid it off early," says Edgar Walker, grandson of John Paxton and longtime Goshen resident. As far as anyone can tell, it was a $9,000 loan that was paid off sometime over the next six years. By the time Mildred left the village, not only had she paid off the loan, but she also had a little money in the bank, which she used to invest in her new business.

❖◆❖―◆❖❖―❖◆❖―❖◆❖―❖◆❖―❖◆❖―❖◆❖―❖◆❖―❖◆❖

She'll Be Home Directly

Michael DiGrassie still remembers the way he pined for his mother when they lived in Goshen. Every evening, he sat at a big window and watched for Mildred. His Aunt Bertha and Uncle Basil cared for him, but it was not the same as having his mother. Sometimes, he stared at a print that hung near the window. It showed a little boy on a raft, with a barn in the background. Underneath the picture were the words "Lord watch over me until my mother comes home."

Often, his grandfather, James Henry Craft, who stayed at their place during his last illness, would say, "What are you doing over there?"

"I am waiting for Mom."

"She'll be home directly," he would reply.

By the time she got home, she was exhausted. Most nights, Michael would be awake just long enough for her to tuck him into bed. Some nights, he drifted off to sleep without her.

❖◆❖―◆❖❖―❖◆❖―❖◆❖―❖◆❖―❖◆❖―❖◆❖―❖◆❖―❖◆❖

Mildred and her two daughters, Brenda and Linda, in their Goshen home.

But he was the father of her children. So, he stood there at the door with her. "Grassi" himself, smart and dapper, could not have known what this moment would eventually mean to the woman he was getting ready to leave behind.

In Goshen, Mildred and her three children, Brenda, Linda, and Michael, shared a huge red brick home with Bertha and her husband, Basil Mays, and their son, Carroll. Basil was a mechanic and he handled the gas station. Mildred and Bertha ran the restaurant, which they called DiGrassie's Grille, together at first. Soon, Mildred ran it alone and Bertha tended the home. This became a pattern in the sisters' lives. In fact, Bertha was really like a second mother to Mildred's children.

About Goshen

A mountain town of about two hundred people, Goshen's history, like many rural towns, is one of high hopes and serious letdowns. Today, Goshen is probably best known for its splendid mountain pass cut by the Maury River.

Bertha and Basil Mays.

*Agnes, Juanita, and Lorraine—the Terry girls of
Goshen—worked for Mildred and remember her
demand for cleanliness and timeliness. The Terry girls
must have passed muster—because not only did they
clean, waitress, and wash dishes at the restaurant, but
they also became Mildred's babysitters and companions
for her children. Mildred loved the girls. She always
used to say, "You can rely on those Terry girls."*

When the restaurant first opened, a customer ordered a cheeseburger. Mildred had no idea what that was. She suggested that he order something else because the "cheeseburger machine" was broken.

Mildred in front of her Goshen restaurant before she remodeled it.

Bertha and Brenda behind the counter at the DiGrassie's Grille (later renamed the Far-Famed).
Michael DiGrassie, Mildred, and Reverend Gentry, a Pentecostal minister, are sitting at the table.

A view of the same Formica counter today.

At first, Eugene visited on the weekends and helped out. After he moved to Florida with the other woman, he stopped visiting on a regular basis. His financial support—or lack of it—of Mildred and their three children is a bit murky. Brenda, the eldest of the children, says she remembers occasional checks from her father; Mildred's sisters, however, say there were no checks. According to letters from lawyers and Eugene himself, Mildred tried to get regular child support payments from him for many years. The last letter is dated 1961.

Though faced with the incredible obstacles that divorced women in the forties and fifties had to deal with, Mildred Craft DiGrassie had two strong things in her favor—her sister Bertha and her brother-in-law, Basil. This was her support system. "I never thought anything of it," says Bertha, shrugging. "We are family. It's what you do for family."

If Mildred had stopped to take a breather and look around her new restaurant, she may have seen a couple in the corner happily eating their meatloaf, or local men sitting at the counter drinking their second cup of coffee, probably talking about

Goshen, Land of Dreams

Just before the turn of the twentieth century, the village was poised for grandeur. And because of the railroads, for a while, it captured that promise. In 1891, Goshen Land and Improvement Company purchased some nine thousand home sites and erected the luxurious Alleghany Hotel in hopes of making Goshen into a large city. It also purchased the already developed Cold Sulfur Springs (built around 1870), which had accommodations for 250 people and a dance hall.

But the sulfur water that was said to be the cure for all did not have enough of a cure to keep folks coming. During World War I, tourism sharply declined. And with the increasing popularity of the automobile, it looked as if the resort that folks came to on a train was doomed. Sometime in the 1920s, Cold Sulfur Springs burned to the ground. It was never rebuilt. In 1923, the palacelike Alleghany Hotel also burned down.

In 1935, Mrs. Eleanor Roosevelt visited Goshen to tour the Stillwater Textile Mills, which were said to be model mills in terms of working conditions. She stayed with Joseph and Pearl Teeter Wood, who owned the home that is now the Hummingbird Inn, a bed and breakfast sitting next to the once-busy railroad tracks.

politics, then sports, then women. She would offer a wisecrack or two, while looking clean and crisp in her snow-white uniform, which set off her coal-black hair.

The new golden-yellow laminate counter that she had purchased was the most modern restaurant equipment—it was called Formica and was said to be indestructible. She also installed some wood paneling to make the place seem more warm and homey, especially to the traveling salesmen who were the mainstay of her business. But more and more, she had noticed, families were coming in, especially families whose kids were at nearby Camp Virginia during the summer. Some of them made it a special point to come back.

When Mildred first opened the Goshen restaurant in 1947, it was a roadside luncheonette. Open only for breakfast and lunch, it was an efficient business, with the counters and grills close by. Many restaurants in that day were only for special occasions and it took a great deal of time and money to eat out. In many cases, the food was French, or some other gourmet or foreign food. The lunch counter was not any of those things, which suited Mildred's personality—efficient, effective, thrifty, and uniquely American.

The Allegheny Hotel in its glory days.

Mildred was in a remarkable position. Because of the increasing popularity of cars and improved roads, a new phenomenon was occurring in America: the roadside restaurant. Americans owned twenty-six million cars at the time and never before had they traveled so easily. Mildred was there and waiting with her home-style food. She also took advantage of the latest kitchen technology. Frigidaire now offered a unit that used Freon, reducing risk of toxic fumes. There was new stainless steel cutlery and cookware, the automatic toaster, the electric mixer, the coffee percolator, homogenized milk, and sliced bread.

"Mildred was one of those rare individuals who really knew people, especially young people. She could tell us things that our parents wouldn't dare say during that period of time. She just had that motherly attitude toward all of us young people and we felt comfortable talking to her about subjects that we probably didn't talk to our parents about."

—EDGAR WALKER, GOSHEN RESIDENT

Soon, DiGrassie's Grille became the Goshen Restaurant. Later, after Mildred established a reputation among travelers, she changed the name to the Far-Famed, after a customer from California suggested it. The Far-Famed is now the Mill Creek Cafe. Mildred leased the business in 1952 when she moved to Staunton after Marrying Willard Rowe, who opened the current restaurant in 1947 and finally sold the Far-Famed in 1956. The knotty-pine paneling is still there from Mildred's days, and so is the golden-yellow Formica counter.

Mildred came to Goshen a stranger with a past. But not only did her restaurant become an eating center, it also established her as one of the townspeople. They still claim her as their own. This was perhaps Mildred's greatest achievement and talent—her charisma and ability to connect with people. This trait, above all

> *"**Mom loved to gamble on football and baseball games. She had no idea what she was doing, of course. And it used to drive the men in her restaurant crazy because she'd win every time. Every time.**"*
>
> —Brenda Hathaway, Mildred's daughter

else, made her the success she was. She would probably disagree with that assessment and say it was her food.

One thing is certain: Mildred found she had more strength and stamina than she had ever realized. Even after Eugene came back and begged her to move to Florida with him, she told him no thanks. Of course she could not find it within herself to forgive him for his infidelity. But it certainly was more than a matter of pride and heartbreak. For now Mildred realized that she could manage and thrive without a husband and this lifted her and stretched her imagination.

Cucumbers and Onions

Mildred's lunch and supper tables included this favored salad. Michael noticed his Uncle Bosie (Virginia's husband) never ate the cukes, so he asked him why. His crisp response: "A hog won't eat cucumbers, so why would I?" Cucumbers from the garden or bought from a local farmer offer the best flavor.

* Combine the cucumbers and onions in a large bowl.

* Combine the vinegar, sugar, and oil in a small saucepan over high heat. Bring to a boil and cook, stirring constantly, for 1 minute, until the sugar dissolves. Pour the vinegar mixture over the cucumbers and onions and stir to coat evenly. Add the salt and pepper and toss well.

* Cover and refrigerate for at least 30 minutes, until chilled. The salad can be served cold or at room temperature.

Serves 4 to 6

2 large cucumbers, or 1 English cucumber, thinly sliced

1 onion, thinly sliced and separated into rings

½ cup apple cider vinegar

4 teaspoons sugar

2 teaspoons vegetable oil

1 teaspoon salt

½ teaspoon freshly ground black pepper

B. B.'s Coleslaw and Dressing

Mildred's sister Bertha is often called B. B. Many of the recipes Mildred relied on came from her sisters, especially Bertha. Watching Mildred and Bertha in the kitchen was like watching a dance, they worked together in an absolutely rhythmic way. Their knowing hands kept busy as if they had a memory of their own and knew exactly what to do—because the women did not often appear to be concentrating. In fact, they continually bickered. As the bickering went in all directions, their hands provided a single meditation. Serve this slaw with your favorite sandwich and potato chips.

✳ Make the dressing by whisking together the vinegar, salt, sugar, mayonnaise, and mustard in a small bowl until the sugar dissolves.

✳ Combine the cabbage, celery, onion, and carrot in a large bowl. Pour the dressing over the cabbage mixture and toss to coat evenly. Serve immediately or store covered and refrigerated for up to 1 week.

Serves 4 to 6

¼ cup apple cider vinegar

½ teaspoon salt

⅓ cup sugar

¼ cup mayonnaise

½ teaspoon yellow mustard

3 cups shredded cabbage

⅓ cup finely chopped celery

⅓ cup grated onion

¼ cup grated carrot

Mandarin Orange Salad

Mildred had a passion for tropical flavors and savory mandarin was one of her favorites. This is a nice salad for brunch.

✱ Preheat the oven to 350°F. Spread the almonds in a single layer on an ungreased baking sheet. Toast, tossing several times, for 5 to 10 minutes, until golden brown.

✱ Combine the lettuces, celery, carrot, green onions, and oranges in a large salad bowl. Cover and refrigerate until chilled.

✱ Make the dressing by combining 2 tablespoons of the reserved orange juice, the oil, vinegar, ketchup, soy sauce, Worcestershire sauce, sugar, garlic, and basil in a jar. Cover tightly and shake until the sugar dissolves. Refrigerate until chilled.

✱ Just before serving, pour the dressing over the salad and toss to coat evenly. Sprinkle with the almonds and serve at once.

Serves 4 to 6

¼ cup slivered almonds

1 small head iceberg lettuce, torn into bite-size pieces

1 head Bibb lettuce, torn into bite-size pieces

3 celery stalks, thinly sliced

1 carrot, shredded

4 green onions, white parts, sliced

1 (11-ounce) can Mandarin oranges, drained, juice reserved

¾ cup vegetable oil

¼ cup white wine vinegar

¼ cup ketchup

1 tablespoon soy sauce

1 tablespoon Worcestershire sauce

⅓ cup sugar

1 clove garlic, minced

1 teaspoon dried basil

Potato Salad

"Aunt Bertha's potato salad was always the best—creamy, sweet, and moist," says Michael. The dressing is used mostly for the potato salad, but its versatility warrants experimenting. Willard always stored it in closed jars in the refrigerator, which would keep it fresh and moist, and then carried them with him to the restaurant. The recipe is so good that Michael dips bread in it for a special treat. You could also try sprinkling it over a pasta salad, mixing it in a cucumber dish, or using it as a sandwich spread.

✳   To prepare the dressing, combine the eggs, sugar, vinegar, and salt in a saucepan over low heat. Stir constantly for 5 minutes, until the dressing thickens. Remove from the heat and allow to cool. Stir in the mustard and mayonnaise.

✳   Bring 6 cups of water to a rolling boil in a large pot over high heat. Add the potatoes and cook until tender when pierced with a fork, but not until falling apart, about 15 minutes. Drain. Combine the potatoes, onion, celery, pimientos, and hard-boiled eggs in a large bowl. Add the dressing and stir to coat evenly. Add the salt and pepper and toss well. Serve immediately or store covered and refrigerated.

Serves 4 to 6

Dressing
Makes about 1 cup

2 eggs, lightly beaten

½ cup sugar

¾ cup apple cider vinegar

Pinch of salt

1 teaspoon yellow mustard

2 tablespoons mayonnaise

2 pounds potatoes, peeled and diced (about 4 cups)

1 onion, chopped

¾ cup chopped celery

1 (4-ounce) jar pimientos, chopped

3 hard-boiled eggs, chopped

1 teaspoon salt

½ teaspoon freshly ground black pepper

Sauerkraut Salad

This is one of Bertha's home recipes that often graced family tables. Michael remembers it as his favorite among the many traditional dishes served at Christmas. "I always ate the leftover salad. It's even better the second day," he says.

✳ Combine the sauerkraut, celery, bell pepper, and pimiento in a large bowl.

✳ Make the dressing by whisking the sugar, vinegar, and oil together in a small bowl until the sugar dissolves. Pour the dressing over the sauerkraut mixture and toss to coat evenly. Cover and refrigerate overnight. Stir well before serving. The salad can be served cold or at room temperature.

Serves 4 to 6

1 (28-ounce) can shredded sauerkraut, drained and rinsed

1 cup sliced celery

1 cup diced green bell pepper

2 (3-ounce) jars pimientos, chopped (about 1 cup)

1½ cups sugar

½ cup distilled white vinegar

⅓ cup vegetable oil

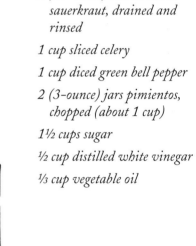

Roscoe Thompson, cook.

Caesar Salad Dressing

Toss with a head of Romaine lettuce and sprinkle with Parmesan cheese. Serve with grilled shrimp or chicken breast.

✳ Combine the egg yolk, lemon juice, wine, Worcestershire sauce, anchovies, garlic, and pepper in the bowl of a food processor and process until smooth. With the motor running, add the olive oil in a slow, steady stream, processing until the mixture is creamy and emulsified. Add the cheese and parsley and pulse to combine. Serve at once or store covered and refrigerated for up to 2 weeks.

Makes about 1½ cups

1 egg yolk

2 tablespoons freshly squeezed lemon juice

2 tablespoons white wine

1 tablespoon Worcestershire sauce

5 anchovy fillets, coarsely chopped

2 cloves garlic, coarsely chopped

½ teaspoon freshly ground black pepper

1 cup extra virgin olive oil

3 tablespoons freshly grated Parmesan cheese

1 teaspoon chopped fresh flat-leaf parsley

Willard's Thousand Island Dressing

Willard's dressing concoction has become a Rowe's specialty. Pour it over your favorite tossed salad or use as a spread for a Reuben sandwich, like the restaurant does.

✳ Mix all of the ingredients together in a bowl until well combined. Store covered and refrigerated for up to 2 weeks.

Makes about 2 cups

1 cup mayonnaise

½ cup chili sauce

2 hard-boiled eggs, chopped

2 tablespoons finely chopped celery

2 tablespoons finely chopped green bell pepper

1 tablespoon finely chopped onion

1 teaspoon paprika

½ teaspoon salt

Staff timecards.

Bread and Butter Pickles

These are the sweet and spicy pickles found on many Appalachian tables.

✳ Combine the cucumbers, onions, and peppers in a large bowl or pot. In a separate bowl, dissolve the salt in the ice water and pour over the vegetables. The vegetables should be completely covered. Let stand for 3 hours and then drain well.

✳ Combine the vinegar, sugar, mustard, turmeric, and cloves in a large pot and bring to a boil over high heat. Add the vegetables and return to just under the boiling point. Do not allow the vegetables to boil.

✳ Ladle the hot pickles into hot, sterilized canning jars, leaving 1 inch of headspace. Seal immediately following the canning instructions on page 61.

Makes 8 quarts

30 unpeeled cucumbers, sliced into thin rings (about 1 gallon)

8 onions, sliced into thin rings

2 large red or green bell peppers, cut into fine strips

½ cup salt

About 8 cups ice water

5 cups distilled white vinegar

5 cups sugar

2 tablespoons mustard seeds

1 teaspoon ground turmeric

1 teaspoon whole cloves

Chow-Chow

Chow-chow is a sweet, pickled relish traditionally made in the South. It's a great way to use up the vegetables left over at the end of the summer's harvest. Many of these recipes have been handed down for generations from mother to daughter or son. "Mother loved to make, can, and eat chow-chow. It was a staple at our house and eaten with pinto beans, fried potatoes, and cornbread," says Brenda Hathaway, Mildred's oldest daughter.

✳ Combine the onion, cabbage, bell peppers and tomatoes in a large, shallow, nonreactive container. Sprinkle the salt over the vegetables and cover the surface completely with ice cubes. Let sit in a cool place for 2½ hours. Drain and discard the liquid, pressing the vegetables to remove as much moisture as possible.

✳ Combine the vinegar, sugar, water, celery seeds, turmeric, and mustard seeds in a large pot over high heat. Bring to a boil and cook, stirring constantly, for 2 minutes minutes, until the sugar dissolves. Add the vegetables and cook, stirring constantly, for 5 minutes, until the mixture returns to a boil.

✳ Ladle the hot vegetables into hot, sterilized canning jars, leaving ½ inch of headspace. Ladle the hot vinegar mixture over the chow-chow, leaving ¼ inch of headspace. Seal immediately following the canning instructions on page 61.

Makes 3 to 4 quarts

1 large sweet onion, chopped

1 small head green cabbage, finely chopped

1 large green bell pepper, chopped

1 large red bell pepper, chopped

4 cups chopped green (unripe) tomatoes

2 tablespoons coarse salt

1 cup apple cider vinegar

1½ cups sugar

⅓ cup water

½ teaspoon celery seeds

¾ teaspoon ground turmeric

¾ teaspoon mustard seeds

Dill Tomatoes

In the early summer, when walking through the Alleghany Highlands, you sometimes catch the distant scent of flowering dill.

✳ Pack the tomatoes three-quarters of the way to the top of 4 1-quart jars. Add the onions, celery, and pepper and tuck them in down the sides with the tomatoes. Place the dill on top of the vegetables.

✳ Combine the water, vinegar, and salt in a saucepan over high heat. Bring to a boil for 5 minutes. Pour the hot liquid over the tomatoes, leaving 1 inch of headspace. Seal immediately following the canning instructions on page 61. After sealing, the tomatoes should be stored at room temperature for 6 weeks before serving.

Makes 4 quarts

2 quarts small green (unripe) tomatoes

2 small onions or garlic cloves, sliced

2 celery stalks, sliced

½ green bell pepper, diced

1 handful fresh dill

2 cups water

2 cups distilled white vinegar

¼ cup salt

Pickled Beets

Imagine biting into a pickled beet in the middle of a harsh Appalachian winter.

✳ Combine the beets and their liquid, the sugar, vinegar, and salt in a bowl. Stir gently until the sugar dissolves. Cover and refrigerate until well chilled for up to 2 weeks. Serve cold.

Makes 1 quart

1 (15-ounce) can sliced beets

½ cup sugar

½ cup distilled white vinegar

Pinch of salt

Lime Pickles

Bertha and Mildred would can or "put-up" enough pickles to last the winter—a fresh, crisp reminder of warm summer days.

✳ Place the cucumbers in a large, nonreactive container or crock. Dissolve the lime in enough cold water to cover the cucumbers. Pour the lime solution over the cucumber slices and place a plate on top so they stay submerged. Let sit in a cool place for 24 hours.

✳ Drain off the lime solution and thoroughly rinse the cucumbers under cold water. Rinse out the container and put the cucumbers back in it. Cover the cucumbers with fresh cold water and let sit in a cool place for 3 hours.

✳ In a bowl, combine the vinegar, sugar, salt, and pickling spices and stir to mix well. Drain the water off the cucumbers and pour in the syrup. Place the plate back over the top of the cucumbers to keep them submerged and let sit in a cool place overnight.

✳ Transfer the cucumbers and the syrup to a large pot and bring to a boil over high heat. Decrease the heat to medium and simmer for 35 minutes.

✳ Ladle the hot pickles into hot, sterilized canning jars, leaving ½ inch of headspace. Ladle the hot syrup over the pickles, leaving ¼ inch of headspace. Seal immediately following the canning instructions on the opposite page.

✳ Variation: For much sweeter lime pickles, follow the above preparation, but use the proportions at right.

Makes 3 to 4 quarts

3½ to 4 pounds cucumbers, sliced into ¼-inch rounds

1 cup pickling lime

1 quart distilled white vinegar

4 cups sugar

1 tablespoon salt

1 tablespoon mixed pickling spices

Sweet Lime Pickles

3½ to 4 pounds cucumbers, sliced into ¼-inch rounds

1 cup pickling lime

3½ cups distilled white vinegar

½ cup water

6 cups sugar

¾ cup salt

2 tablespoons mixed pickling spices

Canning Instructions

1. Check all your jars for nicks and cracks and clean them with hot soapy water.

2. Fill a canning rack with jars and set the rack in a stockpot. Pour in two quarts of water, or enough to cover the jars. Bring to a boil and keep at a rolling boil for at least 15 minutes. Remove from heat and keep the jars in the hot water until they are ready to be filled with food.

3. Prepare the food according to the recipe. Using tongs, remove one jar at a time, dumping the water back into the pot. Using a wide-mouthed funnel, pour the hot food into the jars up to the recommended line. Wipe down the rims of the jars with a damp paper towel. Using tongs, place lids on the jars. Using potholders, tightly screw on each lid.

4. Place the jars upright in the rack in the water. Bring the water to a boil again and boil for 10 minutes.

5. Using the tongs, remove the jars and set them on a wire rack overnight. The lids should create a suctioned seal by morning.

Chapter 4

Soups & Stews

Goshen Days and Blackberries Like Gold

"If you want to eat pie, you better pick the berries."

—Mildred Rowe

Up until the very last year of her life, Mildred used the rhubarb out of her own garden to make pies for the restaurant. She also picked, peeled, and cored apples for her yearly mincemeat pie and apple dumplings. In addition to feeding people, another sustaining passion in Mildred's life was gardening. No matter where she lived—in Covington, Goshen, or Staunton—she always had a patch of land on which she gardened, often using the bounty in the restaurant or giving it away.

The Goshen restaurant and gas station when the Mays and DiGrassies owned it.

Even after her first heart attack, when the doctor gave her strict orders to avoid anything strenuous, she could not stay out of the garden. One day, the eighty-nine-year-old Mildred decided to walk down the steps of her back porch, just to do a little weeding. Soon she had pulled up all the honeysuckle. But the effort was too much for her and she collapsed on the bottom step, gasping for breath. She yelled for Bertha, who was soundly sleeping.

The two bickered about it later.

"Where were you?" Mildred snapped.

"I was napping."

"Why were you napping this time of day?"

"I am ninety-two years old, and I'll nap any time I want to," Bertha told her. "What were you doing out there?"

"Well I just figured as long as I am here, I ought to do some weeding."

From Folk Medicine to Food

A few times, a local forager brought Mildred ramps, an Appalachian onionlike plant, sometimes called wild leeks. Ramp harvest in Appalachia begins around the middle of April. Mildred knew all about them and may have picked them as a child. Much stronger in flavor than onions or garlic, ramps are often used as a folk medicine and are said to keep away colds and flus. Since they are available in the spring, and Mildred's mother was a great user of folk medicine, she may have been given them in a spring tonic. But when the forager brought them into the restaurant, Mildred fried the ramps with mushrooms, kielbasa sausage, and eggs, probably as weekend special.

The local farmers all knew about Mildred's demand for fresh and clean produce. Charmed by it, many of them just gave her whatever she could pick. Many times, farmers would bring bushels of Brussels sprouts, peaches, and apples to the restaurant for her, and would not take a penny in return. Some of these relationships began during her Goshen days and lasted until the end of her life.

Mildred was most passionate about picking blackberries. Both in Staunton and Goshen, she knew of all the best spots for berry picking. Her favorite place was the mountain behind their home in Goshen. Often trailed by a group of children or teenagers, she would scare up rabbits and quail in a field, wade across the clear Calf Pasture River, and snake through stands of towering trees, where squirrels and deer pricked up their ears at the group's approach.

> **"People still bring in garden food for us and we use it.**
> **I don't know if that happens at other restaurants or not."**
>
> —MICHAEL DiGRASSIE, MILDRED'S SON

One day, Mildred, her father, and her nephews Bobby Craft and Carroll, went blackberry picking. After her father killed a rattlesnake, Bobby and Carroll tried to convince her that they should leave—nobody wanted to get bit by a rattler.

"Keep picking berries. You'll hear a rattlesnake before it bites you. Just stay away from it," Mildred said.

"But, Aunt Millie," Carroll protested, "what if there's copperheads? They won't rattle."

"Just make a lot of noise. Snakes will crawl off," she replied.

Mildred reveled in this act of picking berries. Maybe it was because it epitomized the free bounty of the earth and harkened back to the days of her childhood ambition—picking the most, the fastest, and being able to make a little money at it too.

Picking blackberries was not the only aspect of Mildred's food life that she attempted to get all of her family involved in, especially the younger members. Children, either her own, her nephews, or locals, were always in and out of her Goshen restaurant. Balancing her restaurant duties and tending to rambunctious children became an everyday occurrence. Once her nephew Parker drank a whole bottle of ketchup in front of customers. Another time, little Michael wandered off and the whole town began searching for him, only to find him at the railroad station learning Morse code from the station chief.

Mildred sometimes closed the restaurant at 1:00 P.M. on Saturdays and spent the rest of the afternoon with her children. But she usually returned in time for the regular Saturday night restaurant scrub down. Sometimes she and the kids would visit family, or go to Staunton to see movies, or eat at Marino's, a small Italian restaurant that was a favorite of hers. They visited Covington,

> *"Some people have sought adventure in searching for gold. Aunt Millie's gold was a blackberry patch."*
>
> —CARROLL MAYS, MILDRED'S NEPHEW

Juanita Terry, who normally worked at the Goshen restaurant. Here she is in the kitchen of the Far-Famed.

Michael DiGrassie, then seven, remembers his mom's first date with Willard in November 1952. "We were standing on the landing of the stairs and looking out the window, trying to catch a look of him. We couldn't really see him, just his mammoth Oldsmobile. It was the biggest car I had ever seen. That really impressed me."

Willard Rowe and his "mammoth" car.

"I came to Goshen with five dollars in my pocket, and I made a killing."

—Mildred Rowe

Roanoke, and Lexington, but Staunton was the regular, and here Mildred stopped in a time or two to eat at Perk's Barbecue, Willard's place.

When approaching the little town of Goshen heading west, the Mill Creek Grill and gas station sits on the left. Driving past the restaurant, the First Presbyterian Church sits on the left; off to the right is a road that curls up a hillside to the Goshen Baptist Church, where Mildred's family attended church.

The church is white clapboard and small. The mountains fold into one another against the backdrop of the country church. When Mildred lived here, this might have been a place of refuge and strength for her. Thinking of her walking these hillsides, looking for blackberries, taking the time to go fishing or to sit and eat pie with her children is a comforting thought. In reality, those times were lacking in her life then.

The original cash register still sits at the Mill Creek Cafe.

"All I did was work," she has often said about that time.

But things changed for her in 1952 when Willard Rowe started "reeing" (courting) her. In general, Mildred was reluctant to discuss her life in Goshen, but she liked to talk about Willard Rowe, even if it was just to set the record straight. "Willard was a good man, a wonderful husband, and a great businessperson, but he did not sweep me off my feet," she said, indignantly.

It is hard to believe that anybody would or could sweep Mildred off her solidly planted feet. But their romance was a whirlwind, which provided rumors for the locals and even some family members. They said Willard was marrying Mildred for her money. If indeed he was, he probably was pretty disappointed. All that she had, she willingly gave to him. But after her savings were his, that was it. She had nothing else. Nothing, that is, but her culinary and gardening skills, her growing business sense, and, of course, her heart.

Ham and Bean Soup

This is one of Aaron's favorite of the Rowe's signature dishes. It has been on the menu since Mildred owned her restaurant in Goshen. Her mother probably taught her how to make it while growing up in Rich Patch. They could brew a big batch and keep it in the cool cellar for days.

✳   Rinse the beans under cold water. Place the beans in a large, heavy pot and cover with cold water by 2 inches. Stir in the salt. Bring to a boil over high heat and cook for 2 minutes. Remove the pot from the heat, cover, and let stand for 1 hour. Return the pot to the heat and bring to a simmer over medium heat. Cook for about 1 hour, until the beans are tender. Drain off the liquid.

✳   Combine the olive oil, onions, garlic, and 1 cup water in a separate large pot. Bring to a boil over high heat and cook for 10 minutes, until the water evaporates. Stir in the ham, tomatoes, broth, white pepper, cumin, black pepper, and hot sauce. Boil for 10 minutes, until the liquid is reduced by half. Stir in the beans and heat until warmed through. Taste and add more cumin or hot sauce, if needed. Serve at once or cool, cover, and refrigerate for up to 1 week.

Serves 12

2 cups dried beans (such as navy, pinto, or great Northern)

1 tablespoon salt

2 tablespoons olive oil

2 onions, minced

3 cloves garlic, minced

1 cup water

8 ounces baked or boiled ham, diced

2 cups diced fresh tomatoes, or 1 (14.5-ounce) can diced tomatoes, drained

4 cups chicken broth

½ teaspoon freshly ground white pepper

¼ teaspoon ground cumin

¼ teaspoon freshly ground black pepper

Dash of hot sauce

Vegetable Beef Soup

Aaron says his grandmother would cook her soups all day. The aromas filled her home and followed her wherever she went. To this day, when he catches a certain soup smell, he thinks of her.

* Place the beef and bone in a large pot. Cover with water (about 6 cups). Bring to a simmer over medium heat and cook for 30 minutes, until the meat is tender and the broth tastes rich. Remove the meat and set aside. Remove and discard the bone.

* Stir the tomatoes, ketchup, onions, carrot, potatoes, celery, cabbage, bell pepper, green beans, and okra into the broth. Simmer for 1 hour, until the vegetables are tender. Stir in the reserved meat, peas, corn, sugar, seasoned salt, onion powder, garlic powder, Accent, and salt. Simmer for 10 minutes, until warmed through. Taste and add more salt, if needed. Serve at once or cool, cover, and refrigerate for up to 1 week or freeze for up to 6 months.

Serves 12

8 ounces beef, any cut, cut into bite-size pieces

1 meaty beef bone

1 pound fresh tomatoes, peeled, or 1 (14.5-ounce) can diced tomatoes, drained

¾ cup ketchup, or 1 (6-ounce) can tomato paste

2 onions, chopped

1 large carrot, peeled and chopped

2 large potatoes, peeled and chopped

1 celery stalk, chopped

1 cup chopped cabbage

¼ cup diced green bell pepper

½ cup diced fresh green beans

¼ cup sliced okra

1 cup fresh or frozen peas

1 cup fresh or frozen corn kernels

½ teaspoon sugar

½ teaspoon seasoned salt

½ teaspoon onion powder

½ teaspoon garlic powder

½ teaspoon Accent seasoning (includes MSG)

½ teaspoon salt

Soup's on. Homemade Vegetable Beef Soup.

Chicken Noodle Soup

Willard loved soup so much that he ate it nearly every day for lunch. Michael remembers eating chicken noodle soup as a child when he was sick. Unfortunately, he also remembers cod liver oil being offered alongside.

✳ In a small pan over medium heat, cook the chicken breast for 5 to 7 minutes on both sides until opaque when sliced open with a fork. Transfer the chicken to a cutting board. Finely chop and set aside.

✳ Combine the broth, onion, celery, and carrots in a large saucepan. Bring to a simmer over medium-high heat and cook for 2 to 3 minutes, until the vegetables are tender. Add the noodles and cook for 5 minutes, until tender. Stir in the chicken and heat through. Stir in the salt and pepper. Serve at once or cool, cover, and refrigerate for up to 1 week.

Serves 8

1 chicken breast

2 quarts chicken broth

⅓ cup chopped onion

⅓ cup chopped celery

1 tablespoon peeled and finely minced carrots

8 ounces ¼-inch fettucine noodles, broken into short lengths

½ teaspoon salt

¼ teaspoon freshly ground black pepper

Cream of Potato and Bacon Soup

Michael says this is the most popular soup at the restaurant. "I eat it and remember our home in Goshen and the big pots of it that Aunt Bertha made. I still get a feeling of warmth and comfort when I taste it."

✳ Combine the potatoes, onion, celery, and carrot in a large pot over medium heat. Cover the vegetables with water (about 4 cups), bring to a simmer, and cook for 15 minutes, until tender.

✳ Place a skillet over medium-high heat. Add the bacon and cook, turning, until crispy. Transfer the bacon to paper towels to drain, reserving the drippings. Crumble the bacon.

✳ Pour the bacon drippings into the vegetables. Stir in 3¾ cups of the milk. In a small bowl, stir together the remaining ¼ cup milk and the flour to make a smooth paste. Stir the paste into the soup. Simmer the soup for 5 minutes, until thickened. Stir in the salt and pepper. Add the reserved bacon just before serving. Serve at once or cool, cover, and refrigerate for up to 1 week.

Serves 12

4 cups diced potatoes

⅓ cup chopped onion

⅓ cup chopped celery

¼ cup peeled and grated carrot

6 bacon slices

4 cups milk

1 tablespoon all-purpose flour

1 teaspoon salt

½ teaspoon freshly ground white pepper

Old-Fashioned Beef Stew

John Morris, Rowe's longtime cook, now passed, is the originator of this recipe. "John was truly a great Southern cook," says Michael. If you thicken the stew, it can be used for potpie filling or be canned. For some flavor variations, add any or all of the following when you add the hot water: 1 bay leaf, a pinch of dried marjoram, a pinch of dried thyme, 1 minced garlic clove, or 1 teaspoon celery seed.

✳ Combine the flour, 1 teaspoon of the salt, ¼ teaspoon of the pepper, and the paprika in a shallow container. Dredge the beef in the flour mixture, shaking off any excess and set aside in a single layer.

✳ Heat the drippings in a large pot or Dutch oven over medium-high heat. Add the beef and cook, turning, for 2 to 3 minutes, until browned on all sides. Add the chopped onion and sauté for 2 minutes, until softened.

✳ Sprinkle any remaining seasoned flour over the meat and onion. Add enough hot water to just cover the meat. Cover the pot, decrease the heat to low, and simmer for about 2 hours, until the meat is tender.

✳ Add the whole onions, carrots, and potatoes. Cover the pot and simmer for 40 to 50 minutes, until the vegetables are tender.

✳ Stir in the remaining 1 teaspoon salt and ½ teaspoon pepper. Serve at once or cool, cover, and refrigerate for up to 1 week.

Serves 12

2 tablespoons all-purpose flour

2 teaspoons salt

¾ teaspoon freshly ground black pepper

Pinch of sweet paprika

1½ pounds stewing beef, cut into 1½-inch cubes

1½ tablespoons meat drippings, vegetable shortening, or oil

1 onion, chopped

6 small white onions

3 carrots, peeled and sliced

3 potatoes, peeled and diced

Willard's Brunswick Stew

Brunswick Stew, named after the county it was created in, is a Virginia original. In 1828, an African American chef named "Uncle" Jimmy Matthews first put it together, using squirrel. This concoction has varied through the years; chicken is now substituted for squirrel and vegetables have been added. On February 22, 1988, at the state capitol in Richmond, Brunswick County, Virginia, was proclaimed as the Original Home of Brunswick Stew. This variation was found in Willard's little brown notebook. He notes that pouring the lukewarm stew into jars and placing them in the refrigerator is the best way to keep it fresh.

* Place the pork in a large, heavy pot and cover with water. Bring to a simmer over medium-high heat and cook for 1½ hours, until the meat separates easily. Drain the meat and chop into ¼-inch cubes.

* Place the chicken in a large, heavy pot and cover with water (about 3 cups). Bring to a boil over high heat. Decrease the heat to medium-low and simmer for 1 hour, until the chicken separates from the bone. Remove and discard the chicken skin and bones. Return the chicken meat to the pot and stir in the pork. Simmer for 30 minutes.

* Bring another large pot of salted water to a boil over high heat. Add the potatoes and cook for 20 minutes, until tender. Drain and rinse well under running water.

* Add the potatoes, onions, butter beans, peas and carrots, corn, okra, and tomatoes to the meat pot and stir well. Stir in the salt, sugar, bay leaf, and butter and decrease the heat to low. Simmer gently, stirring occasionally, for at least 1 hour, until the broth is thick enough to coat the back of a spoon. Serve hot or cool, cover, and refrigerate for up to 1 week.

Serves 32

12 ounces pork butt

1½ pounds chicken pieces

6 potatoes, peeled and diced

2 small onions, diced

1 cup butter beans or baby lima beans

1 cup frozen peas and carrots, thawed

2 cups fresh or frozen corn kernels

1 cup sliced okra

2 cups diced fresh tomatoes,

2 teaspoons salt

2 teaspoons sugar

1 bay leaf

1 cup unsalted butter

Chili

This recipe was found tucked away in one of Mildred's spiral notebooks on crumbly, yellowed paper. Celery, not a usual chili ingredient, is used here as a flavor enhancer.

✻ Place a large pot over medium-high heat. Add the ground beef and cook, turning and breaking up any clumps, for 5 minutes, until browned. Drain off any grease. Add the tomato juice, bell peppers, onion, and celery and cook for about 8 minutes, until the vegetables soften. Stir in the salt, pepper, chili powder, garlic powder, paprika, and beef base. Cook, stirring occasionally, for 10 minutes.

✻ Stir in the ketchup and continue cooking for about 10 minutes, until the chili thickens. Serve at once or cool, cover, and refrigerate for up to 1 week.

Serves 8

1½ pounds ground beef

2 cups tomato juice

2 green bell peppers, finely chopped

1 onion, finely chopped

3 celery stalks, finely chopped

1 teaspoon salt

½ teaspoon freshly ground white pepper

3 tablespoons chili powder

1½ teaspoons garlic powder

1 tablespoon sweet paprika

2 teaspoons beef base

2 cups ketchup

Salt-cured Virginia country hams.

Perk's Beef Stew

The man who sold Perk's Barbecue to Willard wrote this recipe. The recipe came along with the restaurant when Willard took over. Serve with buttered Hot Rolls (page 8) or Skillet Cornbread (page 12).

✳ Stir the flour, salt, and pepper together in a shallow container. Dredge the beef in the flour mixture, shaking off any excess, and set aside in a single layer.

✳ Heat the shortening in a large, heavy pot or Dutch oven over medium-high heat. Working in batches to not overcrowd the pan, add the beef and cook, turning, for 2 minutes, until browned on all sides. Transfer the meat to a bowl as it is browned. When all of the meat is browned, return it to the pot. Sprinkle any remaining seasoned flour over the meat.

✳ Add enough water to just cover the meat (about 5 cups) and decrease the heat to medium-low. Cover the pot and simmer for about 2 hours, until the meat is tender. Stir in the celery and onion and simmer uncovered for 20 minutes, until the vegetables are tender. Stir in the potatoes and tomatoes and simmer uncovered for 20 to 30 minutes, until the potatoes are tender. Serve at once or cool, cover, and refrigerate for up to 1 week.

Serves 12

¼ cup all-purpose flour

2 teaspoons salt

1 teaspoon freshly ground black pepper

2 pounds stewing beef, cut into bite-size pieces

2 tablespoons vegetable shortening or vegetable oil

5 celery stalks, diced

1 large onion, diced

2 large potatoes, peeled and diced

2 (14.5-ounce) cans diced tomatoes, drained

Willard's Sunday Oyster Stew

When Willard came home on Sunday evenings, Mildred most often had a bowl of steaming oyster stew waiting for him.

✳ Heat the milk in a saucepan over low heat. When the milk begins to steam, stir in the oysters with their liquid and the butter. Simmer gently for about 1 minute, just until the oysters begin to curl at the edges. Stir in the salt, pepper, and paprika and serve at once.

Serves 6

4 cups whole milk

1 pint shucked oysters with liquid reserved

4 tablespoons unsalted butter

1 teaspoon salt

½ teaspoon freshly ground black pepper

Pinch of sweet paprika

Potato Soup with Fried Hot Dogs

Brenda remembers: "We all loved Mother's cream of potato soup with hot dogs. It was always served with wedges of buttered homemade toast."

✳ Combine the potatoes, onion, celery, carrot, salt, and pepper in a large, heavy pot over high heat. Cover with water (about 3 cups) and bring to a boil. Decrease the heat to low, partially cover, and simmer for about 30 minutes, until the potatoes fall apart easily.

✳ Melt the butter in a skillet over medium heat. Add the hot dogs and cook, turning, for about 8 minutes, until browned. Transfer the hot dogs to a plate and pour the drippings into the soup.

✳ Stir 3½ cups of the milk into the soup. In a small bowl, stir together the remaining ½ cup milk and the flour to make a smooth paste. Stir the paste into the soup and simmer for about 20 minutes, until thickened. Season to taste with salt and pepper. Just before serving, stir in the fried hot dogs. Serve at once or cool, cover, and refrigerate for up to 1 week.

Serves 8

4 cups peeled and diced russet potatoes (about 6 potatoes)

1 small onion, chopped

2 celery stalks, sliced

1 carrot, grated

1 teaspoon salt

½ teaspoon freshly ground white pepper

4 tablespoons unsalted butter or margarine

3 hot dogs, sliced into ½-inch-thick rounds

4 cups whole milk

¼ cup all-purpose flour

Sweet Onion Soup

This is one of Aaron's recipes that has passed the test with the customers at Rowe's. Make certain that the onions are completely cooked and translucent. If not, the soup will be lumpy.

✳ Heat the oil in a large, heavy pot over medium heat. Add the onions and garlic and cook, stirring frequently, for about 10 minutes, until the onions are very soft but not browned. Pour in the wine and scrape the bottom of the pan with a spatula to loosen any browned bits. When the wine evaporates, stir in 1½ quarts of the stock and simmer for 15 minutes, until the onions begin to break down and blend with the stock.

✳ Working in small batches, transfer the soup to a blender and purée until smooth, adding more stock if needed. Pour the purée into a clean pot and keep warm over medium heat. Stir in the cream, salt, pepper, and thyme and serve hot.

Serves 12

2 tablespoons olive oil or vegetable oil

12 cups sliced sweet onions (about 12 onions)

2 cloves garlic, chopped

¼ cup dry white wine

1½ to 2 quarts chicken broth or vegetable broth

1 cup heavy whipping cream

2 teaspoons salt

½ teaspoon freshly ground black pepper

½ teaspoon dried thyme

Tomato-Basil Soup

Aaron and Karl Craig, a Rowe's chef, combined efforts to create this soup. They tried to make it with puréed fresh tomatoes, but the fresh tomatoes did not work as well as condensed tomato soup.

✳ Heat the oil in a skillet over medium-high heat. Add the celery, onion, carrot, and basil and cook, stirring often, for about 15 minutes, until the vegetables soften. Transfer the vegetables to the top of a large double boiler set over simmering water. Stir in the soup, cream, and water. Bring to a simmer and cook for 30 minutes, until thick and creamy. Stir in the salt. Serve at once or cool, cover, and refrigerate for up to 1 week.

Serves 8

1 tablespoon olive oil

½ cup diced celery

½ cup diced onion

¼ cup peeled and diced carrot

½ teaspoon dried basil

2 (10-ounce) cans condensed tomato soup

2 cups heavy whipping cream

½ cup water

1 teaspoon salt

Chapter 5

Sides

"Skillet," the Man from Staunton

"I've got my teeth set for fried chicken tonight."

—Mildred Rowe

rom the moment Willard saw her in her Goshen restaurant, Mildred captured his imagination. He almost gasped out loud at her beauty. When he saw what she was doing, he almost gasped again. She was cooking and waitressing to a fairly large breakfast crowd. He probably watched her funny, quick, lean-forward walk, as she undoubtedly flew past him into the kitchen.

Sitting at the counter, Willard could have smelled the bacon and eggs, as well as heard the sizzling and crack of the hot grease as it met with the food. He may have also seen mounds of pancakes, biscuits, and gravy. If he was there for more than five minutes, as he assuredly was, he would have witnessed her cleanliness and the astute and constant wiping of the counters, grills, and tables. She was birdlike in her quick movements, filling mugs with fresh-brewed coffee, placing plates heaped with food in

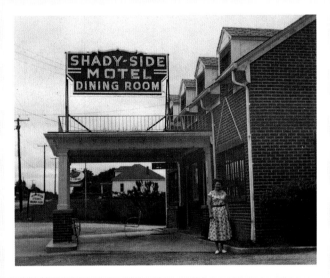

This is a photo of Mildred in front one of the hotels they stayed at on their brief honeymoon.

front of delighted eaters, and always smiling and offering a quick-witted comment or two. He could almost see her thoughts: did anybody need anything?

Sometime during his first visit, the two struck up a conversation. Even though Willard was handsome and had a flirtatious nature, what probably triggered Mildred's interest was finding out that he owned Perk's Barbecue, a roadhouse in Augusta County,

Mildred and Willard stole away for a few days for their honeymoon to Newport News, Virginia.

just outside of Staunton. Beyond that, they had plenty else in common. They both were divorced and knew what they wanted and did not want from a relationship.

Willard could see that the popularity of her little restaurant could only halfway be caused by the food. It was Mildred's charisma that brought in the traveling salesmen, the travelers going back and forth to the Homestead resort, and the families picking up their children at Camp Virginia. That same charisma hooked Willard Rowe.

On May 23, 1953, six months after the couple began courting, Mildred and Willard were married in the way mature couples often do, without fuss and frivolity. They dropped off Brenda, Linda, and Michael at the Dixie Theater in Staunton

Mother Bear Bertha

When Willard asked Mildred to marry him, Bertha reacted with mother-bear instincts. "I told him, 'You may love her, but she's got three kids and I love them. You better be good to them.'" Bertha soon found she had nothing to worry about with Willard. He stepped right in and became a father to Mildred's children.

Two postcards from her honeymoon were saved by Mildred all these years.

Mildred's new home and business. The newlyweds lived in the basement.

An inside view of Perk's—soon to be Rowe's Seafood and Steakhouse.

and stood before Reverend H. G. Craig, also the owner of Dutch Haven, a home for the elderly, and a chicken farm that supplied eggs and chicken to Willard's restaurant. Their marriage was witnessed by Basil and Bertha, who was, as always, standing beside Mildred.

Mildred wore a powder-blue suit, which set off her coal-black hair and green eyes so much that she glowed. Just

A dapper Willard Rowe at his spot behind the register.

after they were married, Willard took Mildred to meet his first wife, Gladys Austin; his daughter, Connie; and Gladys's second daughter, Sonie. The then ten-year-old Sonie Austin remembers the newlywed Mildred: "I don't think I'd ever seen such a beautiful woman."

As Mildred began her new life, she may have faced it with trepidation. Her new husband had a past. She did too. When she married Eugene, Mildred was bright-eyed and full of hope, and gave herself completely to him. When she married Willard Rowe, her hopes shifted to more realistic expectations of a marriage.

After their honeymoon, the Rowes settled in the cramped basement apartment of Perk's Barbecue. Mildred left Goshen, with her big house, sister, and plenty

❖◆❖ ❖◆❖ ❖◆❖ ❖◆❖ ❖◆❖ ❖◆❖ ❖◆❖ ❖◆❖ ❖◆❖ ❖◆❖

The Complaint Department

Mildred's first rule of business was to treat customers like family. And by the time she became Mrs. Willard Rowe, she had mastered the art form of small talk and banter. Once a customer came up to the counter at Rowe's and said, "Where's the complaint department?" "It closed for lack of business," Mildred quipped and the man was taken aback with laughter. She never knew the nature of his complaint—or even if he had one.

❖◆❖ ❖◆❖ ❖◆❖ ❖◆❖ ❖◆❖ ❖◆❖ ❖◆❖ ❖◆❖ ❖◆❖ ❖◆❖

of neighbors behind. She also left her children with Bertha and Basil to finish the school year. Her new home was isolated on the almost desolate rural outskirts of

The waitresses on the floor—Nora Almarode, Danie Jarret, Reba Morris, and two others who could not be identified.

a very small town, Staunton. There were other businesses nearby on Route 250—a farm equipment supply store, a hosiery plant, and Harner's Auto Sales. Customers came from all those places, along with the Woodrow Wilson Rehabilitation Center. On the weekends, she went to Goshen to be with her children and to bask in her friendly Goshen neighbors.

The Rowes had planned to live and work in Goshen, operating the Far-Famed. It was much more successful and, at the time, was located in a better traveled spot. But nobody wanted to buy Willard's restaurant. Mildred, reluctant to let go of her place completely, leased it, and turned her attention to their new business together.

The first thing the couple did was change the name to Rowe's Seafood and Steakhouse; then they added several items to the menu—food that she served her customers in Goshen—fried chicken, meatloaf, pies, and so on. It was all homemade, which, even then, was unique. This was a time that most Americans had gotten used to the modern conveniences of frozen and canned food.

Because the business was a roadhouse, it was open until 11:00 P.M. and would often get rowdy—which did not set well with the new Mrs. Rowe. She put up

"If you missed a day, or a meal, the next time you came in, Willard would want to know where you were."

—FRED BROWN, WHO WAS IN BUSINESS WITH THE HARNERS FOR A WHILE

with it for about a week, then she told her new husband: "Either the drunks go, or I go." They changed their hours of operation, closing at what she considered to be a decent hour, which was 8:00 P.M., and it became a new policy that alcoholic beverages would not be served unless the patron ordered something to eat—a fine example of Mildred's anti-alcohol Baptist background providing a compass for her business decision.

Cleanliness was always important to Mildred, and Willard was a particularly clean man. Jean Harner, a daily customer from the very beginning, said that one of the things Willard was known for was his excellent coffee. One day, she asked him what the trick was. "It's the clean coffeepot," he told her. "I clean the pot three or four times before I make the coffee."

Willard's bent toward extreme cleanliness meshed with Mildred's, though she had probably never gone to an employee's house to see how clean it was before hiring them. Willard did. He would not hire anybody to work in the kitchen unless he had been in their home.

Willard was the youngest in a family of six boys and two girls that grew up in Deerfield, Virginia. He loved to cook and dreamed of having his own restaurant business; he was called "Skillet" by his friends and family. In 1945, he was working at the DuPont plant in Waynesboro making yarn. It was good, steady work, but he

Willard's pride and joy signature 1954 Ford pink station wagon. If employees did not have a ride to work, he'd pick them up and take them home. Willard would also chaperone girls from Staunton's all-girls Mary Baldwin College back and forth to the restaurant. He always made sure to get them home in time for curfew. The girls' grateful parents often stopped in the restaurant as well.

hated it. By that time, with two divorces behind him and child support payments, Willard did not have the capital to start his own business. So, in 1946, he turned to his brother, Hubert, who purchased Perk's Barbecue. Willard then leased it from Hubert.

Before the brothers owned the restaurant, it had a seedy reputation as a pick-up place for soldiers and veterans who were patients at the Woodrow Wilson Rehabilitation Center. It also had a competitor about five hundred yards up the road called the Blinky Moon. Willard faced a challenge as a new business owner. He wanted to attract a better clientele, but his luck would only take a turn for the worse.

> *"Willard kept shoe polish in the back and he'd let you know if your shoes needed shining. He'd also let you know if your hair needed combing."*
>
> —TOOTIE McLEAR, ROWE'S EMPLOYEE FOR MORE THAN THIRTY YEARS

It started with a kitchen fire, and he was forced to move the restaurant into a neighboring, smaller building. After he finally rebuilt and moved back into his space, another dreadful incident happened. A mentally ill patient escaped from the nearby DeJarnette state mental hospital, came into to the restaurant, and smashed it up, just about destroying the place. According to Willard's friend and longtime customer, Fred Brown, Willard attempted to get the state to pay for the damage. It would not. This devastated Willard and led him into his darkest time. After trying to auction off the restaurant and getting no takers, Willard became even more depressed.

Willard was well loved in the community. People wanted to see a decent man like him succeed. His customers and friends saw him building up a hodgepodge of employees for the restaurant and would even provide transportation for them to get to and from work. He employed blacks, whites, and alcoholics. He bailed one employee out of jail frequently. As though they were family, the employees would often cover for one another if they were in trouble.

One time, the restaurant had a party of twenty-five all wanting steak dinners. Willard asked waitress Marion Robertson how it was going. "Fine," Marion said. "I think I have it under control." "Well, good," said Willard, "because you are going to have cook the steaks. The cook is downstairs drunk and passed out."

It was this crew of flawed but hardworking people that Mildred inherited as she began her new life. Transitions like this are not easy for families. Mildred's

Frog Legs and Stockinged Legs

Marion Robertson was one of the Perk's employees who wore many hats in the early years. She did everything from bookkeeping to waitressing to cooking. Once, Willard asked her to make frog legs. "I did it, but he did not tell me the damned things would jump out of the pan."

Willard even noticed at one point that her stockings had a tiny hole in them. "We can't have that," he said. "Well, Willard," she said back to him. "You got no business looking at my legs."

relationship with her two older daughters, Brenda and Linda, became strained. Maybe Mildred did not know how to handle her maturing daughters. Or perhaps, the changes in her life left her emotionally distant in some ways. It very well could have also been weariness; she was still working all the time, cooking in the morning and waitressing in the evening.

"I have always felt that my mother was happiest when she was not married," Brenda says. "She was her own person and could do things the way she wanted to. She didn't have to answer to anybody."

Mildred's taste of hard-won independence in Goshen was a fixture in her personality that Willard Rowe had maybe not counted on. Since she had been such an astounding success, she assumed that they would be true partners in their joint venture. But it was 1952 and, like most married women then, she would find it difficult not to agree with her husband about major decisions. At least that was the case at first. But she soon showed that she would not be silenced about the restaurant. She always participated in the significant business decisions, which, ultimately, was a good thing.

Baked Apples

Almost as good as pie. In fact, Michael says many customers order baked apples for dessert.

* Preheat the oven to 325°F. Butter a large baking dish.

* Arrange the apples in the prepared baking dish. Pour the water around the apples. Sprinkle the apples with the sugar, nutmeg, and cinnamon. Drizzle the melted butter over the apples. Bake for 30 to 45 minutes, until the apples are tender. Serve warm.

Serves 6 to 8

8 apples, peeled, cored, and quartered

⅓ cup water

1½ cups sugar

1 teaspoon grated nutmeg

½ teaspoon ground cinnamon

2 tablespoons unsalted butter, melted

Baked Beans

Bacon adds a hint of authentic smoky flavor.

* Preheat the oven to 425°F. Butter a 9 by 9-inch baking dish.

* Place a skillet over medium-high heat. Add the bacon and cook, stirring often, until it begins to brown. Stir in the onion and bell pepper and continue cooking for 2 minutes, until the bacon is crispy and the vegetables are soft. Transfer to a large bowl.

* Stir in the pork and beans, garlic, ketchup, brown sugar, Worcestershire sauce, salt, pepper, and mustard. Pour into the prepared baking dish and bake for 35 to 40 minutes, until bubbly. Serve hot.

Serves 4 to 6

2 slices bacon, diced

⅓ cup minced onion

⅓ cup chopped green bell pepper

1 (16-ounce) can pork and beans

1 clove garlic, minced

¼ cup ketchup

3 tablespoons brown sugar

1 tablespoon Worcestershire sauce

½ teaspoon salt

Pinch of freshly ground black pepper

¼ teaspoon dry mustard

Baked Macaroni and Cheese

A Rowe classic. Mildred included mac and cheese on her home table, often making it especially for her grandchildren. But she had plenty of macaroni and cheese fans at the restaurant. "My dad used to stop by the Far-Famed just for the macaroni and cheese. When she moved to Staunton, he changed his route so that he could still get it," says Betsy Fultz, a Staunton resident.

✳ Preheat the oven to 350°F. Butter a 9 by 9-inch baking dish.

✳ Cook the macaroni according to the package directions. Drain well and spread half of the macaroni in the bottom of the prepared baking dish. Top with 2 cups of the cheese.

✳ Spread the remaining macaroni over the cheese. Scatter the remaining 1 cup cheese over the macaroni. Pour the milk over it all. Dot the top with butter. Bake for 20 minutes, until hot and bubbly. Serve at once.

Serves 6 to 8

2 cups macaroni

3 cups grated medium sharp Cheddar cheese or Velveeta

¾ cup milk

2 tablespoons unsalted butter

Baked Tomatoes

John Morris, one of the first cooks at the Staunton restaurant, gave Mildred this recipe. It is the same one still used today. The tomatoes are sweet, with a pleasant crunch.

✳ Preheat the oven to 400°F. Butter a 9 by 9-inch baking dish.

✳ Drain the tomatoes, reserving 2 cups of the juice. In a small bowl, combine 2 tablespoons of the tomato juice with the cornstarch and mix to make a smooth paste. Place the remaining juice in a small saucepan. Add the paste to the saucepan and bring to a simmer over low heat, stirring occasionally to dissolve, for 5 minutes, until the juice thickens and looks glossy.

✳ Combine the tomatoes, sugar, salt, and 8 tablespoons of the butter in another saucepan over medium heat. Cook, stirring often, for 2 minutes, until the sugar melts. Stir in the thickened tomato juice and simmer for 5 minutes.

✳ Place the breadcrumbs in a bowl. Melt the remaining 2 tablespoons butter, drizzle it over the breadcrumbs, and toss to moisten. Cover the bottom of the prepared baking dish with a thin layer of the breadcrumbs. Pour in the tomato mixture, then cover with the rest of the breadcrumbs. Bake for about 20 minutes, until the tomatoes are bubbly around the edges and the breadcrumbs are lightly browned. Serve hot.

Serves 4 to 6

2 (14.5-ounce) cans diced
  tomatoes

1 tablespoon cornstarch

½ cup sugar

Pinch of salt

10 tablespoons unsalted butter

3 cups coarse fresh breadcrumbs

Black-Eyed Peas and Greens

Mildred made this dish every New Year's Day. She said it was for good luck. Serve with pork roast or tenderloin.

✳ If using fresh greens, remove and discard the stems. Chop the leaves into 1-inch pieces, then wash and drain. Place in a large pot and cover with water by 2 inches. Cover the pot and bring to a boil over high heat. Cook for 20 to 40 minutes, until tender, depending on the type of greens. Drain well. If using frozen greens, cook according to the package directions and then drain.

✳ Heat the oil in a large skillet over low heat. Add the garlic and cook for about 2 minutes, until it begins to sizzle. Stir in the peas and cayenne and cook for 2 minutes. Stir in the greens and cook for about 5 minutes, until heated through. Season to taste with vinegar and serve hot.

Serves 4

1 pound fresh greens (such as kale, collards, or turnips), or 1 (10-ounce) bag frozen greens

1 tablespoon olive oil

1 tablespoon chopped garlic

1 (15-ounce) can black-eyed peas, drained and rinsed

Pinch of ground cayenne pepper

1 to 3 tablespoons distilled white vinegar

Boiled Cabbage

While working as a nurse for Mildred's father in their Goshen home, Mary-Lydia Graham remembers this treat being left for her from the night before. A DiGrassie family tradition was eating leftover supper the next morning; Mildred did not approve. "Imagine eating cabbage for breakfast!" she once exclaimed.

✳ Bring the cabbage, water, salt, pepper, and sugar to a boil in a large saucepan over high heat. Stir in the drippings. Decrease the heat to medium-low, cover the pot, and simmer for about 30 minutes, until the cabbage is tender. Serve hot.

Serves 4 to 6

1 head cabbage, cored and coarsely chopped

2 cups water

1 teaspoon salt

¼ teaspoon freshly ground white pepper

1 teaspoon sugar

3 to 4 tablespoons drippings from salt pork or ham skins

Corn Pudding

"A country delicacy," says Aaron. "A sweet corn, with a light soufflé-type consistency." Next to the recipe in one of her notebooks, Mildred comments, "Put in a pan and bake until it don't shake." The pudding batter can be covered and refrigerated for up to 1 day, though if the batter is cold, increase the baking time to 55 to 60 minutes.

✳ Preheat the oven to 450°F. Grease an 8 by 8-inch baking dish with nonstick cooking spray.

✳ Combine the corn, milk, flour, and sugar in a large bowl and stir until smooth. Add the salt, nutmeg, vanilla, eggs, and butter and stir until well blended. Pour into the prepared baking dish. Bake for about 10 minutes, until the top browns, then cover with aluminum foil and continue baking for about another 45 minutes, until the pudding is set and a knife inserted into the center comes out clean. Serve hot.

Serves 6 to 8

3 (16.5-ounce) cans creamed corn, drained

2 cups milk

¾ cup all-purpose flour

½ cup sugar

1 teaspoon salt

1½ teaspoons ground nutmeg

1 teaspoon pure vanilla extract

3 eggs, lightly beaten

4 tablespoons unsalted butter or margarine, melted

Creamed Corn

Another creamy country delicacy. Mildred claimed that white pepper was better for the digestion and more pleasing to look at than black pepper.

✳ Drain one can of the corn, but not the other.

✳ Combine both cans of corn (including the remaining liquid), the sugar, salt, pepper, and butter in a large saucepan over medium-high heat. Bring to a boil. Stir the milk and flour together in a small bowl to make a smooth paste. Stir the flour paste into the corn mixture and cook for 15 minutes, until slightly thickened. Remove from the heat and stir in the vanilla. Serve hot.

Serves 4 to 6

2 (14.5-ounce) cans whole kernel corn

6 teaspoons sugar

¼ teaspoon salt

Pinch of freshly ground white pepper

4 tablespoons unsalted butter

¼ cup milk

2 tablespoons all-purpose flour

2 teaspoons pure vanilla extract

Country Cooked Greens

Mildred picked her greens fresh from the grower or from her own garden. Like the mountain women of Rich Patch, Mildred and her children would gather enough greens to fill a thirty-gallon plastic garbage bag for an annual spring tonic. Her recipe was equal parts poke greens, turnip greens, and dryland cress seasoned with salt pork or bacon.

✳   Wash the greens three or four times in a sink filled with fresh water. Drain them each time and rinse the sink to remove the sand before refilling. After the final rinse, drain the greens in a colander and cut into small pieces.

✳   Bring the water, salt pork, salt, pepper, and sugar to a boil in a large pot over high heat.

✳   Stir in the greens. Decrease the heat to medium-low, cover the pot, and simmer for 1 to 2 hours, until the greens are very tender, depending on the type of greens. Add more water if the greens become dry. Drain off any remaining cooking liquid when the greens are done. Serve hot.

Serves 4 to 6

2 pounds fresh greens (such as collards, turnip, mustard, or a combination)

2 quarts water

2 ounces salt pork, diced

1 teaspoon salt

1 teaspoon freshly ground black pepper

1 teaspoon sugar

Candied Yams

Mildred noted in her handwritten recipe book that you can make mashed yams with the leftovers of this traditional dish. Combine your leftovers (or a can or two of yams) in a mixer with spices, extracts, and sugars. The amounts, of course, depend on how much yam you're working with. She suggests adding a bit of corn syrup to the mix, and putting it all in the oven to get "good and hot." Top with marshmallows and pecans and allow to brown.

✳ Turn the oven to 350°F. Butter a large baking dish. Place the canned yams in the baking dish.

✳ Combine the yam syrup, nutmeg, cinnamon, vanilla, lemon juice, brown sugar, and granulated sugar in a saucepan and stir well. Bring to a boil over high heat. Stir in the cornstarch and butter and cook for 5 minutes, until slightly thickened. Pour the syrup over the yams and bake for 30 minutes, until the liquid is thickened and bubbling. Serve hot.

Serves 4 to 6

1 (29-ounce) can yams, drained
   with syrup reserved

½ teaspoon ground nutmeg

¼ teaspoon ground cinnamon

½ teaspoon pure vanilla extract

½ teaspoon freshly squeezed
   lemon juice

¾ cup packed light brown sugar

¼ cup granulated sugar

3 tablespoons cornstarch

½ cup unsalted butter or
   margarine

Fried Green Apples

An example of mountain subsistence food. You can get fried apples at Rowe's any time of the day, but they are most popular as a side with breakfast.

✳ Melt the butter in a large skillet over medium-high heat. Stir in the apples and sugar. Decrease the heat to medium-low, cover the skillet, and cook, stirring occasionally, for about 25 minutes, until the apples are tender. Serve warm or at room temperature.

Serves 4 to 6

4 tablespoons unsalted butter

6 small tart green apples, cored and quartered

1½ cups sugar

Fried Green Tomatoes

A delicate, crunchy, Southern mainstay. Some folks just coat the unripe tomatoes with flour, then fry them. Mildred's recipe is more flavor-packed, especially when made with fatty bacon drippings, which make the tomatoes extra brown and crispy.

✳ Arrange the tomato slices in a single layer on a cutting board and sprinkle with the sugar, salt, and pepper. This should pull quickly out enough moisture for the crumbs to stick to the tomatoes and form a crust. If not, dip each slice in milk before dredging in the cracker crumbs. Set the coated slices aside in a single layer.

✳ Pour the bacon drippings into a large skillet to a depth of 2 inches and place over medium-high heat. Working in batches, add the tomatoes to the skillet and cook, turning once with tongs, for 2 minutes per side, until golden brown on both sides. Be careful not to overcrowd the skillet; you want to leave enough space between the slices to allow the grease to sear the tomatoes, forming a crunchy crust, rather than absorbing the grease, which would result in soggy tomatoes.

✳ Transfer the tomatoes to paper towels to drain and serve hot.

Serves 4 to 6

4 green (unripe) tomatoes, cut into ½-inch slices

1 teaspoon sugar

1 teaspoon salt

½ teaspoon freshly ground black pepper

½ cup milk (optional)

1 cup saltine cracker crumbs or cornmeal

Bacon drippings or vegetable oil, for frying

Green Beans

Mildred was a magnet for stray animals and she took them in. But she did not like groundhogs, especially those that ate her green beans. Once, during a period of time when the family lived at the restaurant, she rented a piece of land about two miles away so that she could have a garden. A certain groundhog was eating her green beans. She sent Michael there one afternoon with his .22 rifle and told him she'd be back for him. In the meantime, the restaurant filled with customers and she was so busy that she forgot about him. Michael says, "It got really dark, so I walked back to the restaurant. Mom asked me where I'd been. I said 'Where were you?' She felt so bad she had forgotten about me. And I never did get that groundhog." If the green beans were not fresh, one of Mildred's tricks was to add a whole onion to the recipe so the beans wouldn't taste like they were out of a can.

✳ String, snap, and wash the fresh beans or drain and rinse the canned beans.

✳ Bring the water and ham hock to a simmer in a large pot over medium heat. Cover the pot and cook for 20 minutes. Add the beans, replace the cover, and cook for 30 minutes, until the pork broth has penetrated the beans so the flavors combine. Stir in the salt, pepper, and sugar. Remove the ham hock and pick off the meat, discarding the bone and fat. Chop the meat and stir it into the beans. Simmer for another 10 minutes. Serve hot.

Serves 6 to 8

2 pounds fresh green beans, or 4 (14.5-ounce) cans green beans

2 quarts water

1 ham hock

1 teaspoon salt

½ teaspoon freshly ground black pepper

¼ teaspoon sugar

Scalloped Tomatoes

Yes, that's tomatoes, not potatoes. Tomatoes are plentiful in the Appalachians so there's a variety of ways to serve them—some traditional, like fresh slices for a salad or a sandwich, some not so traditional, like this resourceful recipe, which uses canned tomatoes.

✳ Preheat the oven to 350°F. Grease a large casserole dish with butter or nonstick baking spray.

✳ Heat the olive oil over medium heat and add the onions and peppers. Sauté until tender, about 5 minutes. In a medium bowl, combine the tomatoes, sugar, breadcrumbs, and 1 cup of the cheese. Add the onions and peppers and stir well. Transfer the mixture to the prepared casserole dish. Spread the remaining cheese on top and bake uncovered for 30 minutes or until golden and bubbling.

Serves 6 to 8

1 tablespoon extra virgin
   olive oil

1 small onion, chopped

½ small green bell pepper,
   chopped

2 (28-ounce) cans whole
   tomatoes

1 teaspoon sugar

1½ cup toasted fresh
   breadcrumbs

1½ cup grated Parmesan or
   Cheddar cheese

½ teaspoon salt

¼ teaspoon freshly ground black
   pepper

Squash Casserole

Brenda Hathaway contributed this recipe to Mrs. Rowe's Favorite Recipes. *Buttered fresh breadcrumbs will bring out the best of the squash in this casserole.*

✳ Preheat the oven to 350°F. Grease a large, shallow baking dish with butter or nonstick spray.

✳ Place a skillet over medium-high heat. Add the bacon and cook, turning, until crispy. Remove the bacon and reserve the drippings. Crumble the bacon.

✳ Place the squash and bouillon in a saucepan and cover with water. Place over medium heat and simmer for about 10 minutes, just until tender. Drain well, transfer to a bowl, and mash with a fork or potato masher. Stir in the bacon, bacon drippings, onions, bell pepper, sour cream, eggs, cheese, and pimiento. Spoon into the prepared baking dish.

✳ Toss the breadcrumbs and melted butter together in a small bowl. Scatter them over the squash mixture. Bake for 50 to 60 minutes, until browned and bubbling. Serve hot.

Serves 4 to 6

2 bacon slices

5 yellow summer squash, diced (about 5 cups)

1 teaspoon beef bouillon powder

2 small onions, grated

1 green bell pepper, chopped

1 cup sour cream

2 eggs, lightly beaten

½ cup grated sharp Cheddar cheese

1 (2-ounce) jar diced pimientos

1½ cups soft fresh breadcrumbs

1 tablespoon unsalted butter, melted

Succotash

This recipe was found in Willard's little brown notebook, which includes handwritten and typed recipes. It also notes reminders of what needed to be done each day. For example, on Monday, clean the register, mirrors, scales, and stool bases. In addition, he lists the duties of the assistant manager, counter manager, dining room manager, and chef and kept daily kitchen lists and instructions on how to clean. One of the most interesting items in the notebook is his time study, in which he notes how long it took certain employees to peel a 100-pound bag of potatoes. Evidently it took Leroy fifty minutes to do that, as well as clean the machines.

✴ Combine all of the ingredients in a large saucepan over high heat. Bring just to a boil, then decrease the heat to low. Simmer, stirring occasionally, for 30 minutes, until tender. Serve hot.

Serves 4 to 6

1 cup fresh corn, or 1 (15.25-ounce) can whole kernel corn, drained

1 cup fresh frozen baby lima beans, or 1 (15-ounce) can baby lima beans, drained

1 cup milk

2 tablespoons unsalted butter

½ teaspoon salt

¼ teaspoon freshly ground black pepper

White Beans

White beans are plentiful in Appalachia. They keep well and are easy to grow. If you cook white beans so long that the pink backbones pop out of them and then add a lot of butter, you have another staple mountain dish—butter beans.

✳ Rinse the beans thoroughly and pick out any small stones or broken beans. Place the beans in a large pot and cover with water by 2 inches. Bring to a boil over high heat and cook for 2 minutes. Remove the pot from the heat and let stand for 2 hours. Drain the beans and discard the cooking water. Cover the beans with fresh water.

✳ Rinse the salt pork and make several cuts through the pork, but not the rind, with a sharp knife. Add the pork, onion, salt, and pepper to the beans. Cover the pot and bring to a boil over high heat. Decrease the heat to medium-low and simmer for 2 to 2½ hours, until the beans are tender. Add more hot water as needed to keep the beans barely covered. (If using a ham hock, remove it and pick off the meat, discarding the bone and fat. Chop the meat and stir it into the beans. Simmer for another 10 minutes.) Serve hot.

Serves 6 to 8

1 pound dried white beans (such as great Northern, navy, or large limas)

2 ounces salt pork, or 1 small ham hock

1 large yellow onion, chopped

1 teaspoon salt

1 teaspoon freshly ground white pepper

Virginia country ham, diced and used to season beans, greens, and soups. It wouldn't be Shenandoah Valley cooking without the salty ham.

Chapter 6

Main Dishes

Making Staunton Home

"I'm as stuffed as a tick."

—Mildred Rowe

Rowe's Seafood and Steakhouse still had the brightly lit jukebox that played the best of country music. Pasty Cline's or Hank Williams's voice was often the musical backdrop to the usual murmurs of private conversation and not-so-private yelps back to the kitchen. The black-and-white tiled floor and the turquoise counters helped set the stage for the country-food-with-attitude that the restaurant was now serving. Mildred's personality permeated the place, spilling over to the other waitresses, as well as customers and, most important, the kitchen.

A precocious Ginger Rowe with her big brother Michael.

Staunton was becoming Mildred's home. If she had taken stock of her life now, her future seemed to be mapped out for her. As Willard Rowe's spouse, she partnered with him in his faltering business. She wanted to be a good wife and homemaker. As always, she wanted to be a good mother to her DiGrassie children, but now she also had a new baby to take care of.

In 1956, Ginger Rowe (LeMasurier) was born to a forty-one-year-old mother and father. Willard doted on her, as did the DiGrassie children, especially Michael, who finally got his chance to be a big brother.

Mildred and her new baby, Ginger.

By this time, the Rowes had built an addition to the restaurant and a spacious apartment above it so that Mildred could manage Ginger, the restaurant, and her other children, Michael and Linda. Sixteen-year-old Brenda was off at nursing school, visiting on breaks.

Things did not go as planned. Before the precocious Ginger could walk, it worked out fine. But once she became mobile, the restaurant became her playground.

In the midst of one busy day, Mildred looked up and saw her baby walking through the restaurant, completely naked. A few minutes later, a bewildered Michael came long, wondering where his sister had gone. He had been babysitting her and she'd sneaked out of the bathroom and downstairs.

Once the children held a funeral for a beloved cat out in front of the restaurant. As they laid Peaches to rest, John Morris, one of the cooks, read from the Bible as the children sniffled and customers stifled their giggles.

Another time, Mildred and Willard discovered that Ginger had crawled out of a window to sit on the porch roof, waving to delighted but concerned customers as they entered the restaurant.

When Ginger was about four, a truck driver found her under his parked truck—she had been chasing a kitten. This was the final incident—managing the restaurant and their new daughter, along with the other children was just not working. The Rowes decided to move "in town" to a home on Westmoreland Drive, which is where Mildred, Willard, and their children lived for many years, then later, where Mildred lived with her sister Bertha.

If Mildred had had any conflicted feelings about not staying home with her children during the Goshen days, she could have resolved them at this point, for Willard insisted that she stay with Ginger. She had a steadfast husband, and the means to be the mother she always wanted to be.

But Mildred found it was not easy. She had thought she wanted to be at home with her children, but she loved the restaurant. This became a

Willard and Ginger.

source of tension between the Rowes. Mildred never stayed away from the business very long, whether Willard liked it or not.

Like many women of her generation, Mildred found herself struggling with her role. Even though her business sense, cooking skills, and energy had worked to save their restaurant, Willard wanted her to be at home. A part of her wanted that too, but she had a fire and a passion that would not subside. Once again, there were no role models for Mildred, or for Willard. He probably could not understand why she wasn't happy at home. She may not have understood it either.

While Mildred was trying to find her way in her new situation, her children were also growing and changing. Brenda was mostly away at school. Michael was a young boy; Ginger, the baby; and Linda, Mildred's second daughter, was a teenager. She ran with a group of friends that would go to one of their basements on Friday nights and drink beer, smoke, and listen to the Supremes.

"I'd come home and throw up. Mom would come to the door and say, 'What's wrong?' I'd say I had a . . . hot dog. She would say to me, 'Why do you get those hot dogs if they make you so sick?' I am sure she knew what I was up to," says Linda.

Mildred had plenty of help keeping an eye on things. Staunton was a small community that watched out for any person's transgression—especially teenaged persons. Just on "general principal," Mildred often stood in Linda's bedroom doorway and glared at her. Linda would cave in and confess what ever meager sin she had

Perk's renovated into Rowe's in 1961, with a spacious family apartment above the restaurant. You can see the screened-in porch on the upper right part of the building. And you can also see how Ginger could have climbed out the window and sat on the roof.

committed. "And I'd say, 'How did you find out? Have you been to that beauty shop again?' Frances Clemmer's beauty shop . . . that's where all our mothers went. Friday afternoon, she'd go and gossip about the teenagers and how awful we were."

But according to Frances Clemmer, she did not allow any gossip in her shop. "It was not a gossip shop. I would not allow it. We talked about hair styles." But then again, that is what she would say. The code of silence between a Southern beautician and her customers is stricter than any doctor-patient or lawyer-client privilege—especially in Staunton.

Staunton is a town that takes its culture and history seriously. And it's a good thing; otherwise, it would have joined the ranks of other small towns, like Goshen, which had been struggling since the shift away from the railroad. Through the efforts of a group of like-minded individuals who came together in 1971, Staunton now stands as a model to any town looking to become a tourist draw, as well as a place to live and work. This group became the Historic Staunton Foundation.

These days, Staunton is a charming, beautiful town, with Victorian architecture and a quaint downtown, with shops like Grandma's Bait and the Bookstack. The buildings are perched on steep hillsides or gently sloping grades. For such a

The modern sign greets travelers right off I-81.

A view of downtown Staunton from Sear's Hill.

small city, it boasts a lively arts community. One of its claims to fame is country music's Statler Brothers. A poster of the original foursome hangs in Rowe's.

The only museum Mildred ever visited is Staunton's Frontier Culture Museum, which sits near the intersection of I-81, I-64, and Route 250. It's an outdoor living

Ginger Rowe at age fourteen in 1972.

history museum that explores the various cultures that made up the original settlements in the area—German, Irish, and English.

Staunton has a keen eye for the future, but is always building on the past and expanding from it. This romance with the past has created a somewhat less than friendly attitude to outsiders—not tourists, mind you, but people who move to Staunton from other places.

Staunton embodies almost all of the clichés you hear about Southern towns—the garden clubs, the historical societies filled with small-town hubris, and the bluebloods that don't care how rich or talented you are, but who your people are and where they are from.

But farther out in Augusta County are the blue-collar factory workers toiling at places like DuPont, Little Debbie, and Hershey Chocolate; the other working-class

Hollering and Hooting

At one horse show, a bee flew up Mildred's dress. She hollered and hooted and Milton Klotz came to her rescue—reaching all the way in to her girdle (in front of everybody there) to fetch the bee. "My dad and Millie never lived that down," says Karen Klotz. Karen's sister, Julie, was Ginger's best friend.

folks; and the farmers, who were always more like Mildred Rowe. She did not have the time or inclination for the society functions of the Staunton elite, except during her horse years, when Mildred necessarily became a part of the well-off "horse crowd," attending all the social events.

Mildred's love of horses was passed down to many family members. She took great pride in her youngest daughter's love of and talent with horses. The walls of their Staunton home were lined with Ginger's ribbons and photos. On horse show days, Mildred would wake early in the morning—usually around four—and ready their trailer, and then she and Ginger, and usually a few friends, would be on the road before sunrise.

The horse show ribbon wall in Mildred's home.

This probably felt like home to Mildred, harkening back to her farm days in Rich Patch. So, as she trudged off to the horse events, and helped with everything, including the mucking out of the stall, Mildred was in one of her elements.

Socially, church was extremely important to the Rowes; they were regular attendees. Mildred joined Willard's reformed Brethren Church, now Saint Paul's United Methodist Church. They kept the restaurant closed on Sundays for many

Paying the Bill

Longtime customer John Sawyer and Mildred flipped a coin for his bill at Rowe's. Mildred won. When it was time for him to pay, he said, "Now Mildred, you know how the church feels about gambling."

"I had just gotten my driver's license when I ran a stoplight at New and Frederick on the way home. When I got there, Mom was standing in the doorway glaring at me. Someone had called her and told her about it and she took the keys. That was the way we grew up. Staunton was small and everybody knew each other."

—Linda Hanna, Mildred's daughter

years. But when they decided in the 1960s to open on Sunday, it was fellow church-goers who came regularly and supported the business.

It became a tradition for many of the locals to stop by the restaurant after church. Mildred and Willard's minister, John Sawyer, would bring his family and half the congregation. He ordered the same thing every Sunday—a sixteen-ounce hamburger steak and fries. This became such a tradition that the Rowes placed it on the menu as the Sawyer Special. The hamburger steak, which is now a simple eight-ounce hamburger with gravy poured over it, is still the most popular item on the menu. Michael Digrassie

Waitresses at Mrs. Rowe's. Marion Roberston is third from the left.

still recalls how John Sawyer would walk through the restaurant and pick food off of others' plates because his own hamburger steak was just not enough for him. "It sounds impolite," Michael says, "but he was such a charismatic and loved person, that people did not mind at all. In fact they would have been insulted if he had not taken a piece of roll or a French fry, as he walked by."

Baked Pork Tenderloin and Gravy

This is one of the bestselling items at the restaurant. About 350 orders are taken for it each week. If you have any leftovers, break the meat up into the gravy and slop it over biscuits for breakfast.

* Preheat the oven to 325°F. Mix ½ cup of the flour, ½ teaspoon of the salt, and the pepper together in a shallow container.

* Dredge the pork in the flour mixture, shaking off any excess, and set aside in a single layer for 10 minutes. Melt the shortening in a large skillet over medium-high heat. Add the pork and cook, turning once, for 2 minutes per side, until browned on both sides. Transfer to a large, shallow baking dish and cover with aluminum foil.

* Pour all but 4 tablespoons of the drippings out of the skillet, leaving any browned bits on the bottom. Place the skillet over medium heat and scrape up the browned bits with a spatula. Whisk in the remaining ½ cup flour and 1 teaspoon salt and cook, whisking constantly, for 5 minutes, until browned and smooth. Remove the skillet from the heat and gradually whisk in the milk and water. Return the skillet to medium heat and simmer, stirring constantly, for 2 minutes, until the mixture is well blended but not thickened. It will thicken during baking.

* Pour the gravy over the pork and bake covered in aluminum foil for 2 hours, until tender. Arrange the meat on plates with the gravy poured over and serve hot.

Serves 4

1 cup all-purpose flour

1½ teaspoons salt

½ teaspoon freshly ground black pepper

8 (½-inch-thick) slices pork tenderloin

½ cup vegetable shortening

1½ cups milk

1½ cups water

Baked Pork Tenderloin with Carrots and Mushrooms

Aaron DiGrassie created this modern twist on a classic recipe. "I played with this about four times before I got it just right," he says.

✳ Preheat the oven to 400°F. Trim the excess fat from the pork. Rinse and pat the meat dry. Butterfly the slices by splitting them down the center with a sharp knife, cutting almost but not completely through. Season with the salt and pepper.

✳ Heat the oil in a large nonstick skillet over medium-high heat. Add the pork and cook, turning once, for 2 minutes per side, until browned on both sides. Transfer to a large, shallow baking dish. Scatter the mushrooms and carrots over the pork.

✳ Combine the soup, sage, and sour cream in a bowl. Fill the soup can with water, pour it into the bowl, and mix well. Pour the soup mixture over the pork, mushrooms, and carrots. Bake for 1 hour, until browned and bubbling. Serve hot.

Serves 4

4 (1-inch-thick) pork tenderloin slices

½ teaspoon salt

¼ teaspoon freshly ground black pepper

1 tablespoon olive oil or vegetable oil

1 pound mushrooms, stemmed and sliced if large

1 pound baby carrots

1 (10.75-ounce) can cream of mushroom soup

½ teaspoon dried sage

½ cup sour cream

Baked Stuffed Pork Chops

"Every time I stop at Mrs. Rowe's, I order the stuffed pork chops and ask for plenty of gravy. It's the only place that makes them just like my mother did," says Bill Shimer of Westernport, Maryland.

✳ Preheat the oven to 325°F. Mix the breadcrumbs, onion, celery, sage, and a pinch each of salt and pepper together in a small bowl. Add just enough broth to make the mixture moist, but not wet.

✳ Cut a slit into the fatty side of each chop, moving the knife back and forth to form a pocket. Stuff ¼ cup of the breadcrumb mixture into each chop.

✳ Mix 1 cup of the flour, 1 teaspoon salt, and ¼ teaspoon pepper together in a shallow container. Make an egg wash by whisking together the egg, mustard, and ¾ cup of the milk in another shallow container.

✳ Heat the oil in a large skillet over high heat. Dip each chop in the egg wash and then coat completely in the flour mixture, shaking off any excess. Place the chops in the skillet and cook, turning once, for 2 minutes on each side, until browned on both sides. Transfer the chops to paper towels to drain, and then place them in a large, shallow baking dish. Cover with aluminum foil.

✳ Pour all but 4 tablespoons of the drippings out of the skillet, leaving any browned bits on the bottom. Place the skillet over medium heat and scrape up the browned bits with a spatula. Whisk in the remaining ½ cup flour and 1 teaspoon of salt and cook, whisking constantly, for 2 minutes, until browned and smooth. Remove the skillet from the heat and gradually whisk in the remaining 1½ cups milk and the water. Return the skillet to medium-low heat and simmer, stirring constantly, for 5 minutes, until the mixture is well blended but not thickened. It will thicken during baking.

✳ Pour the gravy over the chops, cover the dish with foil, and bake for 1½ hours. Remove the foil and bake uncovered for 30 more minutes, until the top is golden brown. Arrange the meat on plates with the gravy poured over and serve hot.

Serves 4

¾ cup soft fresh breadcrumbs

2 tablespoons minced onion

1 tablespoon minced celery

Pinch of dried sage

Salt and freshly ground white pepper

2 to 3 tablespoons chicken broth

4 (1½-inch-thick) pork chops

1½ cups all-purpose flour

1 egg, lightly beaten

1 tablespoon yellow mustard

2¼ cups milk

1 cup vegetable oil

1½ cups water

Barbecue Short Ribs

"The meat is so tender it just falls off the ribs," says Betsy Fultz, a Staunton customer.

✳ Place the ribs, Worcestershire sauce, steak sauce, hot sauce, garlic powder, salt, and pepper in a large pot and add enough water to cover the ribs. Bring to a boil over high heat. Decrease the heat to medium-low and simmer for 1 hour. Drain off the broth (which is excellent used in other gravy or soup recipes).

✳ Preheat the oven to 350°F. Coat a large baking dish with nonstick spray.

✳ Arrange the ribs in the prepared dish. Pour the sauce over the ribs. Bake for about 1¼ hours, until the meat is extremely tender. Serve hot.

Serves 8

8 pounds beef short ribs

¼ cup Worcestershire sauce

1 cup A.1. Steak Sauce

½ teaspoon hot sauce

2 tablespoons garlic powder

2½ tablespoons salt

1 teaspoon freshly ground black pepper

2 cups Short Rib Sauce (page 30)

Roscoe Thompson making barbecue sauce.

Breakfast Tenderloin and Gravy

Mildred grabbed Aaron by the hand one morning and showed him how to make her tenderloin and gravy. "You need to learn how to do this. Nobody else here can." The legacy of this signature dish continues.

✳ Preheat the oven to 350°F. Combine ½ cup of the flour, ½ teaspoon of the salt, and the pepper in a shallow container.

✳ Dredge the pork in the flour mixture, shaking off any excess and set aside in a single layer for 10 minutes. Melt the shortening in a large skillet over medium-high heat. Add the pork and cook, turning once, for 2 minutes per side, until browned on both sides. Transfer the pork to a large, shallow baking dish and cover with aluminum foil.

✳ Pour all but 4 tablespoons of the drippings out of the skillet, leaving any browned bits on the bottom. Place the skillet over medium-high heat and scrape up the browned bits with a spatula. Whisk in the remaining ½ cup flour and ½ teaspoon salt and cook, whisking constantly, for 5 minutes, until browned and smooth. Remove the skillet from the heat and gradually whisk in the milk and water. Return the skillet to medium-low heat and simmer, stirring constantly, for 5 minutes, until the mixture is well blended but not thickened. It will thicken during baking.

✳ Pour the gravy over the pork and bake covered in aluminum foil for about 1½ hours, until the meat is so tender that it falls apart easily. Cut the meat into small pieces and stir it back into the gravy. Arrange the biscuits on plates and spoon the meat and gravy over. Serve at once.

Serves 12

1 cup all-purpose flour

1 teaspoon salt

½ teaspoon freshly ground black pepper

8 (½-inch-thick) slices pork tenderloin

½ cup vegetable shortening

1½ cups milk

1½ cup water

12 warmed Buttermilk Biscuits (page 7), for serving

Chicken-Fried Steak

This is one of the most popular dishes at the restaurant, especially for those who love their meat nice and crispy. The steak can be served with either the Chicken-Fried Steak Gravy or a black pepper gravy, which is just the medium white sauce (page 32) with 2 to 4 tablespoons of freshly ground black pepper added. It will heat your mouth, but not burn it.

✳ To make the gravy, stir together the butter and flour in a small bowl until smooth and well combined. Combine the milk and buttermilk in the top of a double boiler and bring to a simmer over medium heat. Whisk the butter mixture into the simmering milk mixture. Simmer, stirring frequently, for 10 to 15 minutes, until the gravy thickens. Stir in the salt and pepper, decrease the heat to low, and keep the gravy warm over the gently simmering water. Stir well before serving.

✳ Make an egg wash by whisking together the eggs, buttermilk, hot sauce, Worcestershire sauce, and salt in a bowl. Place the flour in a shallow bowl. Dip the steak into the flour, then the egg wash, and back into the flour, gently shaking off any excess. Set aside in a single layer.

✳ Heat the oil in a large skillet over medium-high heat. Add the meat and fry, turning once, for 3 minutes on each side, until cooked through and golden brown on both sides. Transfer to a serving platter, ladle the gravy over the meat, and serve hot.

Serves 6

Chicken-Fried Steak Gravy

½ cup unsalted butter, melted

½ cup all-purpose flour

4 cups milk

½ cup buttermilk

1 teaspoon salt

2 teaspoons freshly ground black pepper

6 eggs

1 cup buttermilk

1 teaspoon hot sauce

1 teaspoon Worcestershire sauce

1 teaspoon salt

½ cup all-purpose flour

6 (4-ounce) pieces cube steak

½ cup vegetable oil

Chicken or Turkey Potpie

Comfort food at its finest. These days Rowe's offers potpies as frozen entrées in addition to those served in the restaurant. Soothing potpies are a great way to use leftovers.

✳ Preheat the oven to 425°F. Butter a large baking dish.

✳ Combine the broth, chicken, onion, corn, peas, and carrots in a large saucepan over medium-high heat. Bring to a boil, then decrease the heat to medium-low. Simmer, stirring occasionally, for 15 minutes, until the chicken is very tender. Stir the flour and water together in a small bowl to make a smooth paste. Stir the paste into the chicken mixture and cook, stirring constantly, for 2 minutes, until thickened. Stir in the salt and pepper and eggs.

✳ Pour the chicken mixture into the prepared baking dish. Arrange the biscuits on top. (If using the pastry, roll the dough out to a thickness of ⅓ inch. Lay the pastry over the filling and press the edges against the side of the baking dish to seal. Cut several slits in the pastry with the tip of a sharp knife to make steam vents.) Bake for about 15 minutes, until bubbly and browned. Remove from the oven and brush with the melted butter. Serve hot.

Serves 6 to 8

8 cups chicken or turkey broth

8 boneless skinless chicken breasts, or 8 boneless skinless turkey breasts, cut into 1-inch cubes (about 8 cups)

¼ cup minced onion

2 cups fresh or frozen corn kernels

2 cups fresh or frozen peas

2 cups diced carrots

½ cup all-purpose flour

½ cup water

1 teaspoon salt

½ teaspoon freshly ground black pepper

3 hard-boiled eggs, chopped

10 unbaked Buttermilk Biscuits (page 7), or ½ recipe unbaked Plain Pie Pastry (page 145)

2 tablespoons unsalted butter, melted

Country-Style Chicken

Michael notes that this is a great way to use leftover fried chicken—if you have any. Ladled over mashed potatoes, biscuits, or rice, this smooth gravy bursts with chicken flavor.

✳ Preheat the oven to 325°F. Butter a large baking dish.

✳ Combine 1 cup of the flour, ½ teaspoon of the salt, and the pepper in a medium brown paper bag. Pour the buttermilk into a bowl. Working 1 piece at a time, dip the chicken pieces into the buttermilk and then drop into the bag. Close the bag and shake gently to coat evenly. Remove the chicken from the bag and shake off any excess flour. Set aside in a single layer.

✳ Over high heat, melt enough shortening in a large, heavy skillet to fill it to a depth of 1½ to 2 inches. Heat the melted shortening until very hot. Add the chicken to the pan without overcrowding. Decrease the heat to medium and cook for about 15 minutes, until the bottom side of the chicken is golden brown. Turn the pieces over and cook for 15 minutes, until the other side is browned. Decrease the heat to low, cover the skillet, and cook for 10 minutes longer, until tender and no longer pink. Remove the chicken from the skillet and place it in the prepared baking dish.

✳ Pour all but 8 tablespoons of the drippings out of the skillet, leaving any browned bits on the bottom. Place the skillet over medium-high heat and scrape up the browned bits with a spatula. Whisk in the remaining 1 cup flour and 2 teaspoons salt and cook, whisking constantly, for 2 minutes, until browned and smooth. Remove the skillet from the heat and gradually whisk in the milk and water. Return the skillet to medium heat and simmer, stirring constantly, for 5 minutes, until slightly thickened. It will continue to thicken during baking.

✳ Pour the gravy over the chicken, cover the dish with aluminum foil, and bake for 45 minutes. Serve hot.

Serves 4 to 6

2 cups all-purpose flour

2½ teaspoons salt

¼ teaspoon freshly ground black pepper

2 cups buttermilk

1 (2½- to 3-pound) fryer hen, cut into 8 pieces

Vegetable shortening, for frying

3 cups milk

3 cups water

Country-Style Steak and Gravy

Mildred loved to cook this steak and gravy for her grandchildren; Wynne DiGrassie Reiner, Michael's daughter, says it is her favorite dish that her grandmother made. Make certain that the meat is only lightly browned before placing it in the oven. For a slightly punchier gravy, add one small sliced onion.

* Preheat the oven to 325°F. Butter a large baking dish.

* Mix together ½ cup of the flour, ½ teaspoon of the salt, and the pepper in a shallow container. Coat the meat in the flour mixture and set aside in a single layer.

* Melt the shortening in a large, heavy skillet over high heat. Add the meat and cook, turning once, for 10 to 15 minutes, until browned on both sides. Transfer the meat to the prepared baking dish and cover with aluminum foil.

* Pour all but 4 tablespoons of the drippings out of the skillet, leaving any browned bits on the bottom. Place the skillet over medium-high heat and scrape up the browned bits with a spatula. Whisk in the remaining ½ cup flour and 1 teaspoon salt and cook, whisking constantly, for 2 minutes, until browned and smooth. Remove the skillet from the heat and gradually whisk in the milk and water. Return the skillet to medium heat and simmer, stirring constantly, for 5 minutes, until slightly thickened. It will continue to thicken during baking.

* Pour the gravy over the meat and bake covered with aluminum foil for 45 minutes. Arrange the meat on plates with the gravy poured over and serve hot.

Serves 6

1 cup all-purpose flour

1½ teaspoons salt

½ teaspoon freshly ground black pepper

6 (4-ounce) pieces cube steak

½ cup vegetable shortening

1½ cups milk

1½ cups water

Creamed Turkey on Biscuits

A fine way of using up Thanksgiving turkey. Chicken and chicken broth can be substituted for the turkey and turkey broth.

✳ Combine the turkey, broth, corn, peas, carrots, onion, and celery in a large saucepan and bring to a boil over medium-high heat. Decrease the heat to low and simmer for 15 minutes. Stir the flour and water together in a small bowl to make a smooth paste. Stir the paste into the turkey mixture and cook, stirring constantly, for 5 minutes, until thickened. Stir in the salt, pepper, and eggs.

✳ Split the biscuits in half and place 2 halves on each plate. Spoon the turkey and sauce over the biscuits and serve at once.

Serves 8

3 cups cubed turkey

4 cups turkey broth

1 cup fresh or frozen corn kernels, thawed

½ cup fresh or frozen peas, thawed

½ cup diced carrots

¼ cup minced onion

¼ cup minced celery

3 tablespoons all-purpose flour

3 tablespoons water

1 teaspoon salt

½ teaspoon freshly ground black pepper

2 hard-boiled eggs, chopped

8 hot Buttermilk Biscuits (page 7)

Fried Catfish

Further south from Staunton, the rivers are full of catfish. This used to be more of a seasonal dish at the restaurant, but now, with fish-farming growing, there is a steady supply so it can be served year-round. Catfish is best when deep-fried and crispy.

✳ Cut any large catfish fillets into 2½-inch-wide strips. Leave any small fillets whole.

✳   In a bowl, combine the eggs, milk, hot sauce, steak sauce, Worcestershire sauce, and lemon juice and stir until well combined. Combine the breading mix, salt, and pepper in a separate shallow container.

✳   Pour enough oil to completely submerge the fish into a large, heavy pot over high heat. (If you'd rather pan-fry the fish than deep-fry it, use only ½ inch of oil.) Dip the fillets into the egg mixture and then coat in the breading mixture, shaking off any excess. Working in batches to not overcrowd the pan, fry the fillets, turning once, for 3 minutes, until golden brown on both sides. Drain on paper towels and serve hot.

Serves 6 to 8

2 to 3 pounds catfish fillets

3 eggs, lightly beaten

8 cups milk

¼ cup hot sauce

¼ cup A.1. Steak Sauce

2 tablespoons Worcestershire sauce

3 teaspoons freshly squeezed lemon juice

¾ cup seafood breading mix

1 tablespoon salt

1 tablespoon freshly ground white pepper

Vegetable oil, for frying

Fried Chicken Livers

An Appalachian treat that exemplifies the need to use every edible part of the animal and to make it taste as good as you can. Mildred would make a gravy from the drippings and spoon it over toast.

✳ Rinse the livers under cold running water and drain thoroughly on paper towels.

✳ Stir the flour, salt, and pepper together in a bowl. One at a time, coat the livers in the flour mixture, shaking off any excess. Set aside in a single layer.

✳ Pour oil into a large, heavy skillet to a depth of ½ inch and place over high heat. One at a time, carefully lower the livers into the hot oil; they usually spatter. Decrease the heat to medium and fry for 20 to 25 minutes, until cooked through and golden brown and crispy on the outside. Drain on paper towels and serve hot.

Serves 4 to 6

16 ounces chicken livers

1 cup all-purpose flour

½ teaspoon salt

¼ teaspoon freshly ground black pepper

Vegetable oil, for frying

Fried Oysters

Christmas mornings would hold an extra delight for Mildred's family for they knew they would be breakfasting in style. They would have fried oysters and Virginia ham along with their eggs, sausage, buttermilk biscuits, fried apples, gravy, and homemade preserves. Fried oysters were Mildred's favorite Christmas treat—something she never had while growing up in Rich Patch. Willard liked fried oysters as well. His own recipe advises, "They should be fried in butter and lard mixed. Not too much butter for it will make the meat fall apart too easily."

✶ Place the crumbs in a shallow container. Beat the egg and milk in a bowl until well combined.

✶ Heat enough oil to float the oysters in a large, heavy pot over medium-high heat. Melt the butter into the oil. Drain a few oysters at a time with a slotted spoon. Dip them into the crumbs, then into the egg mixture, and then back into the crumbs. Lightly press the coating onto the oysters. Working in batches to not overcrowd the pan, carefully lower the oysters into the oil and cook for 1 to 2 minutes, just until they begin to brown. Drain on paper towels and sprinkle with the salt. Serve hot.

Serves 4 to 6

3 cups saltine cracker crumbs or cornmeal

1 egg, lightly beaten

¾ cup milk

Vegetable oil, for frying

4 tablespoons unsalted butter

1 pint shucked oysters

½ teaspoon salt

Beef Liver and Onions

Doing business with Mildred was often a unique experience, according to Phil Grasty, who provided meat for the restaurant in later years. "Mrs. Rowe was always particular about the meat. If the liver was not sliced a certain way, she'd send it back. She said it did not taste the same, and she was right," says Phil. He says that she was always nice about it, but also very firm. He considered that an admirable trait. Frank Clemmer, a meat expert who dealt with Mrs. Rowe for more than thirty years, agrees about how particular she was. "She wanted what we called 'fancy liver.' It had been deveined and all the gristle was taken out. After all these years of working with meat, I can tell you that the way you slice it has nothing to do with anything." Still, he would not have argued with Mildred about that; it would have been pointless. She was convinced that the fancy liver was best and insisted that the butcher cut it sideways.

✳ Season the liver with the salt and pepper. Place 1 cup of the flour in a shallow container. Coat the liver with the flour, shaking off any excess, and set aside in a single layer.

✳ Melt 2 tablespoons of the butter in a large, heavy skillet over medium-high heat. Add the liver and cook, turning once, for 2 minutes, until browned on both sides. Remove from the skillet.

✳ Add 4 tablespoons of the butter to the skillet over medium heat. When the butter is melted, add the remaining 2½ tablespoons flour and cook, whisking constantly, for 1 minute. Whisk in the broth and cook, stirring constantly, for 5 minutes, until the gravy is thick and bubbly. Return the liver to the gravy and simmer for 10 minutes.

✳ Melt the remaining 1 tablespoon butter in a separate skillet over medium-high heat. Add the onions and cook for 2 minutes, until translucent and tender.

✳ Transfer the liver to a serving platter and top with the onions. Serve hot, with the gravy on the side.

Serves 4

1 pound sliced beef liver

1 teaspoon salt

½ teaspoon freshly ground black pepper

1 cup plus 2½ tablespoons all-purpose flour

7 tablespoons unsalted butter

1 cup beef broth

2 large onions, thinly sliced

Mildred's Original Meatloaf

When eighty-eight-year-old customer Edie Jaquith heard that a Mrs. Rowe's cookbook was being written, she exclaimed, "I hope the meatloaf recipe is in it! It's the best I've ever had."

✳ Preheat the oven to 400°F.

✳ Combine all of the ingredients in a large bowl and stir until well mixed. Transfer to a loaf pan and pat into shape. Bake for 45 to 60 minutes, until cooked through and well browned on top. Remove from the oven and let rest in the pan on a cooling rack for 10 minutes before cutting. Serve hot.

Serves 6 to 8

2 pounds ground beef

2 tablespoons yellow mustard

1 teaspoon salt

2 teaspoons Worcestershire sauce

2 teaspoons hot sauce

2 tablespoons A.1. Steak Sauce

⅓ cup ketchup

2 eggs, lightly beaten

½ green bell pepper, finely chopped

½ small onion, finely chopped

1 celery stalk, finely chopped

½ cup fresh breadcrumbs

Old-Fashioned Chicken and Dumplings

When Clara Rowe stopped in at the Far-Famed, she ordered this classic dish. It impressed her so much that she told her son Willard that he needed to visit the restaurant and talk to Mildred. He did, and the rest is history. Homemade dumplings are the key ingredient; they provide the perfect texture for catching the broth and flavor.

✳ Place the chicken in a large, heavy pot. Cover with the water and add the salt. Bring to a simmer over medium heat and cook for about 45 minutes, until tender. Add the onion and cook for 15 minutes. Transfer the chicken to a platter and cover with aluminum foil to keep warm. Strain the broth through a fine-mesh sieve. There should be about 3 quarts. If not, add enough canned broth to make 3 quarts. Return 2 quarts of the broth to the pot and keep at a simmer over low heat.

✳ Pour the remaining 1 quart broth into a large saucepan and heat to a simmer over medium heat. Stir in 1 cup of the milk. In a small bowl, stir together the remaining ½ cup milk and the flour to make a smooth paste. Stir the flour paste into the broth mixture and cook, stirring occasionally, for 5 minutes, until thickened. Add the chicken and cook for 3 minutes, until heated through.

✳ To make the dumplings, stir the flour, baking powder, and salt together in a large bowl. Cut in the shortening with a pastry blender until the mixture is crumbly. Stir in the egg and enough milk to make a stiff dough. On a floured work surface, roll the dough out to ¼ inch thick. Cut into 2 by 3-inch round pieces. Add to the 2 quarts simmering broth and cook for 10 to 15 minutes, until they float, indicating that they are cooked through.

✳ To serve, ladle the chicken, gravy, and dumplings into bowls and enjoy at once.

Serves 6 to 8

1 (4- to 5-pound) stewing hen, cut into 8 pieces

3½ quarts water

1½ teaspoons salt

1 large onion, chopped

Canned chicken broth, if needed

1½ cups milk

½ cup all-purpose flour

Dumplings

2 cups all-purpose flour

2 teaspoons baking powder

1 teaspoon salt

2 tablespoons vegetable shortening

1 egg, lightly beaten

¼ to ½ cup milk

Oven-Broiled Barbecue Chicken

Michael says to use Rowe's famous Short Rib Sauce (page 30) for some of the best barbecued chicken you've ever tasted.

✳ Preheat the oven to 400°F.

✳ Arrange the chicken pieces in a large shallow baking dish and brush with the melted butter. Season with the salt and pepper. Bake for 20 minutes, until tender and no longer pink. Pour the sauce over the chicken. Decrease the oven temperature to 350°F and bake for another 15 minutes, until the sauce is dark brown but not burnt. Serve hot.

Serves 4 to 6

1 (2½- to 3-pound) roasting
   hen, cut into 8 pieces

2 tablespoons unsalted butter,
   melted

1 teaspoon salt

½ teaspoon freshly ground black
   pepper

1 cup Short Rib Sauce
   (page 30)

Pork Barbecue

This is the recipe that Willard and his mother, Clara, traveled to North Carolina to find. It has been used at the restaurant for more than fifty years. The sauce is a typical North Carolina–vinegar based one—tangy and sweet.

✳ Place the meat in a large, heavy pot and cover with water. Bring to a simmer over medium-high heat and cook for 1½ hours, until the meat separates easily. Drain the meat and chop into bite-size pieces, or the desired consistency.

✳ Place the chopped meat in a large container. Stir in enough barbecue sauce to make the meat very moist. Cover the container and refrigerate overnight. Before serving, place the meat in a large saucepan and heat, stirring occasionally, over medium heat for 10 minutes.

Serves 10 to 12

4 pounds Boston pork butt,
   trimmed of excess fat and cut
   into 2-inch pieces

2 cups Pork Barbecue Sauce
   (page 29)

Pot Roast with Vegetables and Gravy

A traditional Sunday dinner item in the region. The smell of pot roast would linger in the air for hours before it was ready, proving the perfect anticipation for a Sunday meal. Often, women would place it in the oven before church so the family would come home to the delicious aroma.

✳ Rinse the roast and pat it dry. Combine the garlic powder, seasoned salt, and 1 teaspoon of the pepper in a small bowl. Rub the spices over the meat.

✳ Heat the oil in a large, heavy pot or Dutch oven over high heat. Add the meat and cook, turning, for 2 minutes, until seared on all sides. Pour 2 cups of the water around the meat. Place the onions on top of the meat.

✳ Decrease the heat to low, cover the pot tightly, and simmer for 1½ to 2 hours, until the meat is very tender. Add the potatoes and carrots, replace the lid, and continue simmering for 30 minutes, until the vegetables are tender.

✳ Remove the pot from the heat. Transfer the roast and vegetables to a serving platter and cover with aluminum foil to keep warm. Measure the cooking liquid left in the pot. There should be about 3 cups. If not, add enough water to make 3 cups. In a small bowl, mix together the flour and remaining ½ cup water to make a smooth paste. Whisk the flour paste into the cooking liquid. Place over medium heat and cook, whisking constantly, for 5 minutes, until the gravy is smooth and thick. Stir in the salt and remaining ½ teaspoon pepper. Serve the roast and vegetables hot, with the gravy on the side.

Serves 6 to 8

4 pounds chunk roast

1 teaspoon garlic powder

1 teaspoon seasoned salt

1½ teaspoons freshly ground black pepper

3 tablespoons vegetable oil

2½ cups water

3 onions, quartered

6 potatoes, peeled and halved crosswise

6 carrots, peeled and halved crosswise

2 tablespoons all-purpose flour

1 teaspoon salt

Salmon Cakes with White Sauce

For many years, Mrs. Rowe's Restaurant offered this menu item on Friday nights, along with BBQ short ribs. Lines of people often snaked outside the restaurant door. Mildred did not like to see the discomfort of her customers as they waited, though she was delighted at her food's popularity.

✳ Pick through the salmon to remove and discard the skin and bones. Place the cleaned salmon in a bowl and flake with a fork. Stir in the onion, celery, egg, ½ cup of the breadcrumbs, pepper, parsley, and lemon juice. Mix the remaining ½ cup breadcrumbs and the flour in a shallow container. Form the salmon mixture into 8 patties, 1-inch thick and 2-inches wide. Coat the patties with the breadcrumb mixture. Set aside in a single layer.

✳ Over medium-high heat, melt enough shortening to cover the bottom of a large, heavy skillet. Working in batches as necessary, add the patties and cook, turning once, for 2 to 3 minutes on each side, until golden brown on both sides. Transfer to paper towels to drain. Serve hot with the white sauce alongside.

Serves 4 to 6

1 (15.5-ounce) can pink
  salmon, drained

½ cup grated onion

¼ cup finely minced celery

1 egg, lightly beaten

1 cup fine dry breadcrumbs

¼ teaspoon freshly ground white
  pepper

1 tablespoon dried parsley flakes

1 tablespoon freshly squeezed
  lemon juice

½ cup all-purpose flour

Vegetable shortening, for frying

2 cups Thick White Sauce,
  warmed (page 33)

Squirrel and Gravy

While the family lived in Goshen, Brenda says they ate a lot of game—venison, rabbit, and squirrel. "Venison was cooked like beef; rabbit was disjointed, floured, and fried; and squirrel was stewed with a white gravy. I wouldn't eat it now but it was delicious with hot buttered biscuits and fried apples." During the time they lived at the restaurant in Staunton, Michael would sit on their flat roof and shoot squirrels. "Mom would have someone at the restaurant clean it for us and we'd have squirrel that night. She loved eating and cooking it."

* Combine the flour, salt, and pepper in a shallow container. Coat the squirrel pieces in the flour mixture, shaking off any excess, and set aside in a single layer.

* Heat the oil in a large skillet over medium-high heat. Add the squirrel and cook, turning, for 2 minutes, until browned on all sides. Transfer to a plate.

* Pour all but 2 tablespoons of the drippings out of the skillet. Stir in the water and the milk and bring to a boil over high heat. Return the squirrel to the skillet, decrease the heat to low, and cover the skillet. Simmer for about 1 hour, until the meat is tender. Remove the squirrel from the pan, pick the meat off the bones, and stir it back into the gravy. Serve hot.

Serves 4 to 6

½ cup all-purpose flour

1 teaspoon salt

½ teaspoon freshly ground black pepper

2 cleaned squirrels, cut into serving pieces

6 tablespoons vegetable oil

1 cup water

1 cup milk

Southern Fried Chicken

When you order fried chicken at Rowe's, you can expect to wait at least 35 to 45 minutes because it is cooked fresh to each and every order.

✳ Combine the flour, salt, and pepper in a medium brown paper bag. Pour the buttermilk into a bowl. Working 1 piece at a time, dip the chicken pieces into the buttermilk and then drop into the bag. Close the bag and shake gently to coat evenly. Remove the chicken from the bag and shake off any excess flour. Set the pieces aside in a single layer.

✳ Over high heat, melt enough shortening in a large, heavy skillet to fill it to a depth of 1½ to 2 inches. Heat the melted shortening until very hot. Add the chicken to the pan without overcrowding. Decrease the heat to medium and cook for about 15 minutes, until the bottom side of the chicken is golden brown. Turn the pieces over and cook for 15 minutes, until the other side is browned. Decrease the heat to low, cover the skillet, and cook for 10 minutes longer, until tender and no longer pink. Serve hot or cold.

Serves 4 to 6

1 cup all-purpose flour

½ teaspoon salt

½ teaspoon freshly ground white pepper

2 cups buttermilk

1 (2½- to 3-pound) fryer hen, cut into 8 pieces

Vegetable shortening, for frying

Wing Dings—small pieces of fried chicken, crispy on the outside, juicy on the inside—are a favorite among Mrs. Rowe's senior patrons.

Stuffed Green Peppers

These peppers are so good that Michael Digrassie can't control his craving for them—even though he knows they might give him heartburn. Any leftover sauce can be slopped over mashed potatoes, steak, or hamburgers.

✳ To make the sauce, combine the sugar, hot sauce, steak sauce, Worcestershire sauce, salt, pepper, ketchup, and 2¾ cups of the tomato juice in a large saucepan over medium-high heat. Bring to a simmer, stirring constantly. In a small bowl, mix together the remaining ¼ cup tomato juice and the cornstarch to make a smooth paste. Stir the paste into the sauce and cook, stirring constantly, for 5 minutes, until the sauce thickens.

✳ Preheat the oven to 375°F. Coat a baking dish large enough to hold the peppers upright with nonstick cooking spray. Spread about ¼ cup of the sauce in the bottom of the prepared baking dish.

✳ Cut off the tops of the peppers and remove the seeds. Bring a pot of salted water to a boil over high heat. Add the peppers and parboil for 5 minutes. Remove the peppers and let them drain upside down on paper towels.

✳ In a large bowl, combine the ground beef, celery, onion, mustard, ketchup, egg, hot sauce, steak sauce, Worcestershire sauce, salt, pepper, and garlic salt and breadcrumbs and stir until well mixed. Divide the stuffing evenly among the peppers. Stand the peppers upright in the baking dish. Pour the remaining sauce over the peppers. Bake for 45 to 50 minutes, until the beef in the peppers is no longer pink. Serve hot.

Serves 4 to 6

Stuffed Pepper Sauce

¼ cup sugar

2 teaspoons hot sauce

2 teaspoons A.1. Steak Sauce

2 teaspoons Worcestershire sauce

2 teaspoons salt

1 teaspoon freshly ground white pepper

¼ cup ketchup

3 cups tomato juice

1 tablespoon cornstarch

6 green bell peppers

1 pound ground beef

⅓ cup chopped celery

⅓ cup chopped onion

1 teaspoon yellow mustard

¼ cup ketchup

1 egg, lightly beaten

1 teaspoon hot sauce

1 teaspoon A.1. Steak Sauce

1 teaspoon Worcestershire sauce

1 teaspoon salt

1 teaspoon freshly ground white pepper

½ teaspoon garlic salt

½ cup soft fresh breadcrumbs

Virginia Country Ham with Redeye Gravy

This recipe harkens back to the Appalachian tradition of using what you have on hand. Coffee was cheap and plentiful and, like many families, Mildred's kept it going all day long on the woodstove. This recipe is a mild version of a Southern favorite—farther south, spicier pepper is added. Virginia country ham is salt-cured and hung in the open air for up to six months to draw moisture out and enhance its flavor.

✳ Trim off and discard the ham rind. Trim off and reserve all but a small amount of the fat from around the edge of each slice. Score the trimmed fat to keep it from curling as it cooks. Scrape the ham with the backside of a knife. Rinse the ham and pat it dry.

✳ Place a large, heavy skillet over medium-low heat. Add the scored fat pieces and cook for 5 minutes, until they render their drippings. Add the ham and cook, turning several times, for 4 minutes, until lightly browned on both sides but still juicy, not crispy. Remove and discard the pieces of fat. Transfer the ham to a platter and cover with aluminum foil to keep warm.

✳ Pour the coffee into the skillet and bring to a boil over high heat, scraping the bottom of the skillet with a spatula to loosen the browned bits. Decrease the heat to low and simmer, stirring frequently, for 4 to 5 minutes, until slightly thickened. Spoon the gravy over the ham and serve hot.

Serves 6

6 (¼-inch-thick) slices Virginia country ham

1 cup strong brewed coffee

Chapter 7

Pie

Culinary Life Force

"You can tell if someone has given up on life by looking at their shoes."

—Mildred Rowe

oon after Mildred and Willard moved to their brick ranch home on Westmoreland Drive, it was filled with Mildred's presence. She was buoyant, always mobile. Neighbors could see her working in her suburbanish yard, tending her flower and vegetable gardens, as if she were on a farm. If a neighbor stopped to talk, she'd tilt her head and knit her brows and tell them all about her rhubarb crop or her tomatoes. Often, she'd advise them what to do with their gardens, food, or children.

She carried her mountain wisdom with her and was eager to share it. Whether she was in the garden or at the stove, she infused each process with a sense of magic. She'd dip her hands in something, sprinkle a little here or there, then she'd smell it, taste it, and usually exclaim, "Ohhh," and her eyes would get as big and joyful as a child's when opening a gift.

She was also known in the neighborhood for hosting the best birthday parties. But of course she did not wait for a special occasion to feed the neighborhood kids. She became so involved with Ginger and her friends that they called her "Mama Millie."

Soon, Mildred's grandchildren and grown children came in and out of her home on a daily basis. At one point, all of her grown children lived within three blocks of her. She made sure that everyone understood that they were welcome at her table. She never knew who would be there for lunch or dinner, so she'd simply cook enough for everyone— just in case. She was at her most jovial when cooking for a group.

Mildred and Willard going out on the town, a rare occasion. Willard never wanted to leave the restaurant.

It probably felt like being at the restaurant full-time. At this point, during the 1960s, she still went in, greeted customers, and tested the food, sometimes driving Willard crazy because he could not get her out. Talking to the customers was what she loved and what she excelled at. If she didn't know you, she still made you feel as if she did.

Mildred on a rare break from the restaurant, with Ginger beside her. Mildred was not much of a leisure reader, but she loved newspapers. She would read any paper from cover to cover; her favorite was Staunton's Daily News Leader.

Mildred and Willard stayed the course with their vision of the restaurant and its food. Consistency of the food and service saw them through the popularity of canned vegetables and frozen foods, along with a shift to more health-conscious fare. As their following grew, they were visited by a stroke of luck so massive that Mrs. Rowe's Restaurant and Bakery would never be the same.

In 1967, Interstate 81 was completed, placing Rowe's right at the most direct exit to Staunton. The planners even designed the freeway so it would go around the beloved restaurant.

It was never Mildred's way to want to expand the business. She was extremely conservative with her money and wanted to have it in the bank, not invested. But even by 1960, they had a growing clientele and the word was out about the interstate coming through. They could see that if

"Willard did not like to leave the business. I tried to get him to go fishing or hunting with me. We'd get there and a few hours later, he wanted to go back."

—Marion Harner, Staunton resident

they were going to succeed, they would have to expand. So, they added a small dining room and renovated the existing one.

Mildred snoozing with Ginger.

As it turned out, it was a good thing the Rowes had prepared for growth with the expansion there was now room for new clientele coming from the interstate. It was Willand's pushing and planning that opened the way for this expansion.

Tragically, even though Willard saw some success, he would not be there to see the restaurant's greatest success. In 1970, he was diagnosed with colon cancer. He worked as long as he could during his illness, but he died in 1972. Mildred tended to her sick husband as much as possible, while also stepping in and taking over the restaurant.

Ginger was sixteen when her father died, and often remembers her Saturday afternoons with him. He would take a break from the restaurant, come home, and watch wrestling on television with her. He would meticulously corkscrew-peel an apple, eating the fruit and letting Ginger have the peel. "I always think about it and wish he had eaten the peels because who knows, it may have helped him," she says.

The family gathers at the restaurant. The far left is Brenda, then Michael, Willard, Mildred, Ginger, and a friend.

Mildred was surrounded by her family, friends, and customers as she grieved. But even though Willard's two-year illness had prepared her, she still felt lost.

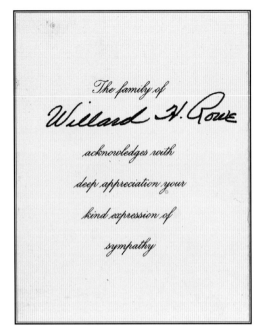

The thank-you note that Mildred sent to people for contributing to the cancer society in memory of Willard. Soon, the restaurant would be the first in the area to be completely smoke-free.

The man who changed her life was now gone and everything would change again, drastically.

Until Willard's illness, Mildred and Willard's working relationship had been tense. She could not stand being away from the business and he did not want her there. Perhaps it seemed to him that she was second-guessing him as she offered suggestions. Perhaps this situation frustrated Mildred because, after all, she did know what she was talking about. Also, she had thought from the beginning that they would be partners in this business. The term "silent partner" is not a concept Mildred understood or embraced.

She finally got her chance to run the restaurant, but at great personal loss, and she knew she could not keep up the pace forever. This restaurant was already a much larger place than the one she ran in Goshen. Mildred needed help. But which family member to turn to?

Michael was studying engineering at Virginia Tech; Linda had just married and had had no interest in the business; Ginger was in high school; and Brenda was settled in South Carolina, with a management position at BlueCross BlueShield of South Carolina, children, and a husband. But it was Brenda who came to her mother's help.

"My sister, Anne, and I used to go to Moo-Moo's house every day after school since both my mom and stepdad worked full time, and we usually stayed for dinner. If Moo-Moo wasn't working that night, she and B. B. would both cook dinner, bickering as is their custom. You never knew who would show up . . . sometimes there were twenty people there."

—SARAH HARRISON, WHO NOW LIVES IN BOSTON

For about fifteen years, Brenda poured herself into the family business. During these years, the restaurant grew. Brenda was hoping to finally capture her mother's approval, but ironically, the more she took over the day-to-day operations, the more strained their relationship became. There were times when they would argue and not speak to one another for weeks. Mildred and Brenda had strong personalities and different ideas about the business. Brenda had modern ideas, for example, and wanted to redecorate the restaurant with more contemporary flair. Mildred agreed to a sprucing up with new menus and a new logo, but would have no contemporary flair.

Brenda's strong will extended into her dealings with the employees at the restaurant. Once, she even broke up a knife fight in the kitchen. At issue was fried chicken; one of Rowe's talented cooks was famous for it, but she also had a bad temper and a drinking problem. Another kitchen employee tried to tell her something about the way she was frying the chicken. The cook lost her temper and came after the other employee with a butcher knife. Brenda broke it up, grabbing the knife out of the cook's hands.

Perhaps more than anything, Brenda's move back to Staunton benefited her daughters, Anne and Sarah. They often stayed with their grandmother—affectionately called Moo-Moo—during the afternoon after school.

During this time Michael graduated summa cum laude from Virginia Polytechnic Institute with a degree in engineering, and he invited his long-lost biological father, Eugene DiGrassie, to attend the event. Much to everybody's surprise, Eugene actually came.

Eugene had remarried and was living in Florida. When Michael was exploring his options as an engineer, he went to Florida and reconnected with his father who then arranged several meetings with some of the biggest developers in the state for Michael. Eugene's passion was real estate as well.

Having watched her children move away from her and establish their own lives, and having said good-bye to Willard, Mildred was faced with running a rapidly growing restaurant mostly alone—until Brenda moved back. It was about this time that she closed the restaurant on Sundays. She felt she just could not do it seven days a week. Mildred may have had an inkling then that Rowe's was poised for even more success.

Once a local doctor was holding a function at the restaurant and asked if he could furnish the meat. Evidently, he had gotten a deal on it. Against her better judgment, Mildred allowed it. It was some of the worst meat the restaurant had ever served. Hence, another one of Mildred's business rules—don't let customers bring their own meat.

Of course, having Jane and Michael Stern as a couple of fans did not hurt the business. In 1986, the restaurant was written up in their *Roadfood and Goodfood*, a guidebook to good restaurants across the United States. The book helped the restaurant reach a whole new customer base. Of course it was already a mainstay with the locals and travelers through the state of Virginia. But now people who loved food and who specifically traveled for food experiences, knew about Rowe's.

The Sterns focused on Rowe's banana pudding. They also raved about the mincemeat pie, the pork chops, and the mashed potatoes. "We could go on and on, dish by dish, but suffice it to say that anything you order at Rowe's will be good regional fare prepared with culinary skill close to genius."

In 1998, the Sterns wrote again about the restaurant—this time in *Gourmet* magazine. In this article, they said that visiting with Mrs. Rowe is "an encounter with a culinary life force that makes the world go round."

Even though by this time Mildred was not doing much of the cooking, it always seemed like she was. The food was that personal. If Mildred did not oversee the making of the food herself, however, the staff never knew when she would taste it, which kept them on their toes.

Once, a cook came upon a case of instant mashed potatoes left by an eager salesman. He figured he could use them instead of taking the time to make the real potatoes: peeling, boiling, mashing, mixing. Within minutes, Mildred was on to him. She stormed into the kitchen, threw the instant potatoes into an outside dumpster, and promptly fired the cook. This is the one time she lost her temper and could not hide it from the customers who happened to be outside the restaurant at the time. So this story has taken its place in the trove of local tales about her.

Mildred's preference for doing things the country way was ingrained into the staff—in one way or another. She moved through the seasons the same way her whole life. Beginning in Rich Patch, when her survival depended on it, her reverence and knowledge of gardens, the seasons, nature, and what to do with fresh foods was a huge part of her personality. Certain seasonal dishes became expected by her family and her customers—apple dumplings, mincemeat pie, blackberry cobbler, apple butter, and so on.

> *"Fried chicken, oven-baked country-style steak with gravy, pot roast, baked ham, biscuits, green beans, mashed potatoes, rice with chicken gravy, B. B.'s Alabama biscuits (which are really dinner rolls), sweet Silver Queen corn, baked macaroni and cheese, fried potatoes, Moo-Moo's spaghetti sauce—this is the fare of my childhood."*
>
> —SARAH HARRISON, MILDRED'S GRANDDAUGHTER

> *"When I worked at the restaurant during the summers, she would come in in the morning. At that time, she would inspect all the produce. I was taken aback at how sharp she was. I just marveled at her. I am very proud of her. She always worked herself to the bone."*
>
> —ANNE FINLEY, MILDRED'S GRANDDAUGHTER

Mildred's passion was not for everyone, though she desperately wanted to see the restaurant stay within her family. Brenda remarried and her interest in the business faded, though she continued to partner with Michael for several years. Now, it seemed that Michael was the only one of Mildred's children who wanted to continue in the business. And only one of her eleven grandchildren's obsessions became food—a little boy who never even knew Willard Rowe. Much later, Aaron DiGrassie, Michael's son, worked his way through culinary school and restaurants in Italy and New Mexico, then was surprised to find himself back home, learning in his grandmother's kitchen.

Plain Pie Pastry

"It takes practice," Mildred would say about any of her doughs. Too much flour will make the dough tough—use just enough to keep it from sticking to the rolling pin.

✳ Sift the flour and salt together into a bowl. Cut in the shortening with a pastry blender until it is the size of small peas. A tablespoon at a time, sprinkle the milk over a part of the flour mixture, gently toss with a fork, and push to the side of the bowl. Repeat until all of the flour is moistened.

✳ Form the dough into 2 equal balls, then flatten into disks. Use at once or cover and refrigerate for up to 2 weeks. On a lightly floured surface, roll out each ball to a thickness of ⅛ inch.

✳ To prebake an empty crust, preheat the oven to 400°F. Press 1 piece of the dough into a 9-inch pie plate and bake for 10 minutes, until firm and lightly browned.

Makes two 9- or 10-inch crusts

2 cups all-purpose flour

1 teaspoon salt

⅔ cup vegetable shortening

5 to 7 tablespoons cold milk

Vinegar Pie Crust

The vinegar doesn't add any flavor, it is simply there as a stabilizer, making this crust easier to manage than the Plain Pie Crust.

✳ Sift together the flour and salt in a bowl. Cut in the shortening with a pastry blender until it is the size of small peas. Add the vinegar, egg, and just enough ice water to moisten the dry ingredients.

✳ Form the dough into 2 equal balls, then flatten into disks. Use at once or cover and refrigerate for up to 2 weeks. On a lightly floured surface, roll out each ball to a thickness of ⅛ inch.

✳ To prebake an empty crust, preheat the oven to 400°F. Press 1 piece of the dough into a 9-inch pie plate and bake for 10 minutes, until firm and lightly browned.

Makes two 9-inch crusts

2 cups all-purpose flour, sifted

½ teaspoon salt

1 cup plus 1 tablespoon vegetable shortening

1½ teaspoons distilled white vinegar

1 egg, lightly beaten

4 to 6 tablespoons ice water

Mrs. Rowe's Meringue

A classic, fluffy version of meringue. You must use a chilled metal bowl with the mixer and add the sugar very slowly.

✳ Place the egg whites and cream of tartar in a chilled metal bowl. Using an electric mixer on slow to medium speed, beat until soft peaks form.

✳ One tablespoon at a time, add the sugar and continue to beat until stiff but not dry peaks form. Pile lightly over a pie, spreading to the edges. Bake according to the pie recipe instructions.

Makes enough to cover one 9-inch pie

4 egg whites, at room temperature

¼ teaspoon cream of tartar

3 tablespoons sugar

Weepless Meringue

An easier, less puffy, and less particular meringue recipe, this recipe can be substituted anywhere Mrs. Rowe's Meringue is used. The trick here is in the cooking of the sugar and water until it is like a sugar-jell.

✳ In a saucepan over low heat, stir together the cornstarch, 2 tablespoons of the sugar, and enough hot water to make a smooth paste. Bring to simmer and cook, stirring constantly, for 5 minutes, until thickened and clear. Remove from the heat and allow to cool.

✳ In a bowl, combine the egg whites and salt. Using an electric mixer on medium speed, beat until soft peaks form. Beat in the cornstarch mixture. One at a time, add the remaining 6 tablespoons sugar and continue to beat until stiff but not dry peaks form. Pile lightly over a pie, spreading to the edges. Bake according to the pie recipe instructions.

Makes enough to cover one 9-inch pie

1 tablespoon cornstarch

8 tablespoons sugar

¼ to ½ cup hot water

3 egg whites, at room temperature

Pinch of salt

Apple Pie

Any firm, tart apple works for this pie, though Staymans or Granny Smiths are best.

✳ Preheat the oven to 450°F. Line a 9-inch deep-dish pie plate with 1 piece of the dough, leaving an inch of overhang.

✳ In a large bowl, combine the 1 cup sugar, the flour, salt, cinnamon, and nutmeg and stir well. Add the apples, sprinkle them with the lemon juice, and toss to coat with the flour mixture. Fill the crust with the apple mixture and dot with the butter slices. Place the other piece of dough on top, crimp the edges, and trim off any excess dough. Cut six 2-inch slits in the top crust for steam vents. Sprinkle the 1 teaspoon sugar over the top. To prevent the edge of the crust from getting too brown, gently fold a strip of aluminum foil around the crimped edge.

✳ Decrease the oven temperature to 350°F and bake the pie for 55 to 60 minutes, until the apples are tender and the crust is golden brown. Remove the foil during the last 10 minutes of baking. Remove the pie from the oven and brush the top with the melted butter. Transfer to a wire rack to cool. Serve warm or at room temperature.

Makes one 9-inch pie

1 recipe Plain Pie Pastry or Vinegar Pie Crust, unbaked (page 145)

1 cup plus 1 teaspoon sugar

2 tablespoons all-purpose flour

Pinch of salt

1 teaspoon ground cinnamon

1 teaspoon ground nutmeg

7 tart apples, peeled, cored, and sliced

1 tablespoon freshly squeezed lemon juice

2 tablespoons unsalted butter, thinly sliced

2 tablespoons unsalted butter, melted

Buttermilk Pie

This old-fashioned pie offers a creamy filling, with a texture similar to egg custard, but a tangier flavor. It bakes loose and needs to sit after cooking to firm up. As it firms, it will develop a skin that will delight children as well as grown-ups who remember with fondness homemade warm pudding skins.

✳ Preheat the oven to 325°F. Line a 9-inch pie plate with the dough and crimp the edges.

✳ In a bowl, combine the butter, sugar, and flour and stir well. One at a time, add the eggs, mixing well after each addition. Add the buttermilk and vanilla and stir well.

✳ Pour the batter into the pie crust. Bake for 25 to 30 minutes, until a thin knife inserted into the center comes out clean. Transfer to a wire rack to cool for 15 minutes, until the filling firms up. Serve warm, at room temperature, or chilled.

Makes one 9-inch pie

½ recipe Plain Pie Pastry or Vinegar Pie Crust, unbaked (page 145)

1 cup unsalted butter, melted and slightly cooled

1 cup sugar

½ cup all-purpose flour

3 eggs

1 cup buttermilk

1 teaspoon pure vanilla extract

Butterscotch Pie

This comforting sunset-orange filling is baked in a crusty pie shell and is optionally decorated with meringue and butterscotch chips or chocolate chips. For a stronger flavor, use dark brown sugar; for a delicate flavor, use light brown sugar.

✳ Preheat the oven to 325°F.

✳ In a small bowl, stir together the egg yolks, brown sugar, cornstarch, and enough water to make a smooth paste.

✳ Place the milk in the top of a double boiler set over simmering water. When the milk begins to steam, slowly whisk in the egg mixture. Cook, stirring occasionally, for about 4 minutes, until thickened. Remove from the heat and stir in the butter and vanilla.

✳ Pour the filling into the crust and bake for about 30 minutes, until golden brown. Transfer to a wire rack to cool. Serve at room temperature or chilled.

Makes one 9-inch pie

3 egg yolks

1 cup packed brown sugar

¼ cup cornstarch

½ to ¾ cup cold water

3 cups milk

1 tablespoon unsalted butter

2 teaspoons pure vanilla extract

½ recipe Plain Pie Pastry or Vinegar Pie Crust, prebaked in a deep dish (page 145)

Cheese and Cream Apple Pie

This is a hallmark Mildred dish that Ginger and Linda remember from their childhood. Ginger often begged her mom to make it. Finally, Mildred confessed that she had lost the recipe. But when she was preparing for Mrs. Rowe's Favorite Recipes, *Mildred went through shoeboxes to sort recipes and "Glory be! She found my favorite apple pie recipe," says Ginger.*

✳ Preheat the oven to 375°F. Line a 9-inch pie plate with 1 dough round, leaving an inch of overhang. Cut the other dough round into long 1-inch-wide strips.

✳ In a small bowl, combine the flour and the 1 tablespoon sugar and sprinkle over the bottom crust.

✳ In a bowl, combine the 1 cup sugar, apples, nutmeg, and cheese and stir well. Pour the filling into the crust. Pour the half-and-half over the filling.

✳ Using the dough strips, make a crisscross pattern for a latticed top crust. Crimp the edges. Bake the pie for 30 to 35 minutes, until the apples are tender and the crust is lightly browned. Serve warm or at room temperature.

Makes one 9-inch pie

1 recipe Plain Pie Pastry or Vinegar Pie Crust, unbaked (page 145)

1 tablespoon all-purpose flour

1 tablespoon plus 1 cup sugar

5 cups peeled, cored, and diced York or Stayman apples (about 5 apples)

½ teaspoon ground nutmeg

8 slices American cheese, diced

1 cup half-and-half

Chocolate Meringue Pie

This concoction is one of Rowe's most popular menu items. Staunton resident and longtime customer Dot Woodrum gets one every year for Christmas. Once, during the confusion of a restaurant renovation, a baker mixed vinegar into the chocolate instead of vanilla. Soon after Dot picked up her pie, her phone rang. A frazzled Michael DiGrassie was on the other end: "Ms. Woodrum," he said. "Don't eat that pie." Dot says, "I remember Mike feeling really terrible because evidently someone had come in from Richmond or Roanoke and bought a pie from the same batch, but he didn't know them, so he couldn't reach them." Willard made a very similar chocolate pie with less sugar and vanilla. His pie was chilled, with no meringue.

✳ Preheat the oven to 325°F.

✳ In a small bowl, stir together the egg yolks, sugar, cocoa powder, cornstarch, and enough water to make a smooth paste.

✳ Place the milk in the top of a double boiler set over simmering water. When the milk begins to steam, slowly whisk in the egg mixture. Cook, stirring occasionally, for about 4 minutes, until thickened. Remove from the heat and stir in the butter and vanilla.

✳ Pour the filling into the pie crust. Top with the meringue. Bake for about 30 minutes, until golden brown. Transfer to a wire rack to cool. Serve at room temperature or chilled.

Makes one 9-inch pie

3 egg yolks

1 cup sugar

¼ cup cocoa powder

¼ cup cornstarch

½ to ¾ cup water

3 cups milk

1 tablespoon unsalted butter

2 teaspoons pure vanilla extract

½ recipe Plain Pie Pastry or Vinegar Pie Crust, prebaked in a deep dish (page 145)

1 recipe Mrs. Rowe's Meringue (page 146)

Lemon Meringue Pie

A tart treat, topped with sugary mounds.

✳   In a small bowl, stir together the cornstarch, flour, and enough cold water to make a smooth paste. Place the egg yolks in a separate bowl.

✳   Bring the hot water, sugar, 1 teaspoon of the lemon juice, and 1 teaspoon of the lemon zest to a boil in the top of a double boiler set over boiling water. Stir in the cornstarch mixture and cook, stirring constantly, for about 15 minutes until smooth and thick. Whisk a little of the hot lemon mixture into the egg yolks and then stir the yolks into the double boiler. Cook, stirring constantly, for 10 to 15 minutes, until thickened. Remove from the heat and stir in the remaining lemon juice and lemon zest, and the butter. Set aside to cool completely, stirring occasionally.

✳   Pour the filling into the crust. Top with the meringue. Bake for about 30 minutes, until golden brown. Transfer to a wire rack to cool. Serve at room temperature or chilled.

Makes one 9-inch pie

3 tablespoons cornstarch

2 tablespoons all-purpose flour

3 to 5 tablespoons cold water

3 egg yolks, lightly beaten

2¼ cups hot water

1¾ cups plus 3 tablespoons sugar

Juice of 1½ lemons

Grated zest of 1½ lemons

1 tablespoon unsalted butter

½ recipe Plain Pie Pastry or Vinegar Pie Crust, prebaked (page 145)

1 recipe Mrs. Rowe's Meringue (page 146)

Pies ready for meringue topping.

Mincemeat Pie

❧

Every year, Mildred and usually Michael went to a local orchard to pick York apples. Michael says, "The mincemeat-making was always supervised by Mother, who was very exact about her recipe and the ingredients used." Because of the seasonality of the ingredients, she always made extra to give away to friends. Michael suggests unpasteurized apple cider, if you can get it from a reliable source. It can carry bacteria if the apples are not properly washed, but it adds an extra zip.

✳ To make the mincemeat, season the beef with the salt and pepper. Place in a large pot over medium-low heat and cover with water. Simmer for 45 minutes, until tender. Remove from the heat and allow to cool.

✳ Using a meat grinder, coarsely grind the beef, suet, apples, and citron. Place in a large bowl and stir in the raisins, currants, brown sugar, cider, cinnamon, nutmeg, cloves, allspice, and lemon juice. Pack tightly into sterilized jars. Refrigerate for at least 4 weeks before using. The mincemeat can be stored in the refrigerator for up to 6 months.

✳ Preheat the oven to 375°F. Line a 9-inch deep-dish pie plate with 1 dough round, leaving an inch of overhang.

✳ Fill the bottom crust with 2½ cups of the mincemeat and cover with the other round of dough, crimping to seal the edges. Make several cuts in the top crust for steam vents. Bake for 35 to 40 minutes, until the crust is golden brown. Remove from the oven and brush the top with the melted butter. Transfer to a wire rack to cool. Serve at room temperature.

Makes one 9-inch pie

Mincemeat

Makes about 3 quarts

1 pound lean beef chunks

1½ teaspoons salt

1½ teaspoons freshly ground black pepper

8 ounces beef suet

2½ pounds York or Stayman apples, peeled, cored, and sliced

4 ounces citron

1¼ pounds raisins

1 pound currants

1 pound brown sugar (2½ packed cups)

3 cups unpasteurized apple cider

1 tablespoon ground cinnamon

1½ teaspoons ground nutmeg

1½ teaspoons ground cloves

1½ teaspoons ground allspice

Juice of 1 lemon

1 recipe Plain Pie Pastry or Vinegar Pie Crust, unbaked (page 145)

2 tablespoons unsalted butter, melted

Old-Fashioned Egg Custard Pie

Most customers under the age of fifty have never heard of egg custard pie. It's like crème brûlée without the sugar crust on top. Instead, maple syrup can be drizzled on top.

✳ Preheat the oven to 350°F. Line a 10½-inch pie plate with the dough and crimp the edges.

✳ In a bowl, combine the sugar, eggs, nutmeg, and vanilla and stir well. Add the milk and stir until well blended. Pour the filling into the crust and dust with nutmeg.

✳ Bake for about 45 minutes, until firm around the edges and the custard has a Jell-O–like consistency. Transfer to a wire rack to cool. Serve at room temperature or chilled.

Makes one 10½-inch pie

½ recipe Plain Pie Pastry or Vinegar Pie Crust, unbaked (page 145)

1 cup sugar

5 eggs

Pinch of ground nutmeg, plus more for the top

2 teaspoons pure vanilla extract

4 cups milk

Original Coconut Cream Pie

Mildred adjusted Goshen resident Clara Cronk's recipe into her own version, which is still being served today. This is the most popular dessert in the restaurant. "You could eat it every day," says Aaron.

✳ Preheat the oven to 325°F.

✳ In a small bowl, stir together the egg yolks, sugar, cornstarch, and enough water to make a smooth paste.

✳ Place the milk in the top of a double boiler set over simmering water. When the milk begins to steam, gradually stir in the egg mixture. Cook, stirring occasionally, for about 4 minutes, until very thick. Remove from the heat and stir in ¾ cup of the coconut, the vanilla, and the butter.

✳ Pour the filling into the pie crust and top with the meringue. Sprinkle the remaining ¼ cup coconut over the meringue. Bake for about 30 minutes, until golden brown. Transfer to a wire rack to cool. Serve at room temperature or warm for a special treat.

Makes one 9-inch pie

3 eggs yolks

1 cup sugar

¼ cup cornstarch

¼ to ½ cup water

3 cups milk

1 cup sweetened flaked coconut

2 teaspoons pure vanilla extract

1 tablespoon unsalted butter

½ recipe Plain Pie Pastry or Vinegar Pie Crust, prebaked (page 145)

1 recipe Mrs. Rowe's Meringue (page 146)

Peanut Butter Pie

Peanut butter was one of the first packaged foods available in the Appalachians. This is a favorite, creamy pie for children. It's especially great when topped with extra whipped cream.

✳ In a bowl, combine the peanut butter and confectioners' sugar and stir well. Reserve ¼ cup and spread the rest in the bottom of the crust.

✳ In a saucepan, combine the flour, the ½ cup granulated sugar, salt, milk, and egg yolks over high heat. Bring to a boil and cook, stirring constantly, for 5 minutes, until thickened. Remove from the heat and stir in the butter and vanilla. Pour the filling into the crust and set aside to cool.

✳ Combine the cream and the 2 tablespoons granulated sugar in a bowl and whip until soft peaks form. Spread the whipped cream over the filling. Sprinkle the reserved peanut butter mixture over the top. Serve at room temperature or chilled.

Makes one 9-inch pie

⅓ cup peanut butter

½ cup confectioners' sugar

½ recipe Plain Pie Pastry or Vinegar Pie Crust, prebaked in a deep dish (page 145)

⅓ cup all-purpose flour

½ cup plus 2 tablespoons granulated sugar

⅛ teaspoon salt

2 cups milk

2 egg yolks, lightly beaten

2 teaspoons unsalted butter

1 teaspoon pure vanilla extract

1 cup heavy whipping cream

Pineapple Cream Pie

Willard Rowe's little brown book gave us this fabulous and unique recipe. It's on the menu at the restaurant from time to time. One customer always calls a few days in advance of his visit and requests that they serve it. "We make sure that we do," says Michael.

✳ Combine the pineapple and ½ cup of the sugar in a saucepan over medium heat.

✳ In a small bowl, stir together 1 tablespoon of the cornstarch and 2 tablespoons of the water to make a smooth paste. When the pineapple begins to simmer, stir in the cornstarch mixture and cook, stirring constantly, for 5 minutes, until thickened. Remove from the heat.

✳ Bring the milk to a simmer in a large saucepan over medium heat. In a bowl, stir together the remaining ¾ cup sugar, the remaining 4 tablespoons cornstarch, the egg yolks, and the remaining 2 tablespoons of water to make a smooth paste. When the milk begins to simmer, stir in the egg yolk mixture a tablespoon at a time and cook, stirring constantly, for 5 minutes, until thickened. Remove from the heat and stir in the pineapple mixture, vanilla, and butter. Set aside to cool to room temperature.

✳ Scrape the filling into the pie crust and refrigerate for at least 1 hour, until chilled. Serve cold.

Makes one 9-inch pie

1 cup fresh or canned crushed pineapple, drained

1¼ cups sugar

5 tablespoons cornstarch

4 tablespoons water

3 cups milk

3 egg yolks

1 teaspoon pure vanilla extract

1 tablespoon unsalted butter

½ recipe Plain Pie Pastry or Vinegar Pie Crust, prebaked (page 145)

Pineapple Meringue Pie

Mildred's love of tropical flavors, mixed with her use of cornstarch, makes this recipe unique. Sprinkle pecans over the pie for added flavor and texture.

* Preheat the oven to 300°F.

* In a bowl, combine ¼ cup of the sugar and the eggs yolks and whisk well.

* Place the pineapple and its juice in a saucepan and heat over medium-high heat. In a bowl, stir together the remaining ¼ cup sugar, the cornstarch, and salt. When the pineapple begins to simmer, stir in the sugar mixture and cook, stirring constantly, for 5 minutes, until thickened. Stir in the egg yolk mixture a tablespoon at a time and cook, stirring constantly, for 1 minute. Remove from the heat and stir in the lemon juice. Set aside to cool to room temperature.

* Scrape the filling into the pie crust and top with the meringue. Bake for about 30 minutes, until golden brown. Transfer to a wire rack to cool to room temperature and then refrigerate for at least 1 hour, until chilled. Serve cold.

Makes one 9-inch pie

½ cup sugar

3 egg yolks

1 (20-ounce) can crushed pineapple, undrained

2½ tablespoons cornstarch

¼ teaspoon salt

1 tablespoon freshly squeezed lemon juice

½ recipe Plain Pie Pastry or Vinegar Pie Crust, prebaked (page 145)

1 recipe Mrs. Rowe's Meringue (page 146)

Rhubarb Pie

Rhubarb was Mildred's favorite plant. She would carry on detailed conversations about her lovingly cared for rhubarb patch, which still grows at her home in Staunton. This big, leafy plant grew freely in the Appalachians. Once again, here is a piece of home that Mildred carried with her.

✳ Preheat the oven to 350°F. Line a 9-inch pie plate with the dough and crimp the edges.

✳ In a bowl, combine the eggs, sugar, butter, and flour and stir until well mixed. Stir in the rhubarb. Pour into the pie crust and bake for about 1 hour, until golden brown. Transfer to a wire rack to cool. Serve at room temperature or chilled.

Makes one 9-inch pie

½ recipe Plain Pie Pastry or Vinegar Pie Crust, unbaked (page 145)

2 eggs, lightly beaten

1 cup sugar

1 tablespoon unsalted butter, melted

1 tablespoon all-purpose flour

2 cups thinly sliced rhubarb stems

Strawberry-Rhubarb Pie

The strawberries add sweetness to this otherwise tart treat.

✳ Preheat the oven to 400°F. Line a 9-inch pie plate with 1 dough round and crimp the edges.

✳ In a large bowl, combine the sugar, flour, salt, and nutmeg and stir well. Stir in the rhubarb and strawberries and let sit for 20 minutes. Pour the filling into the bottom crust and dot with the pieces of butter.

✳ Cover the filling with the other round of dough and crimp the edges to seal. Cut several steam vents in the top crust. Bake for 40 to 50 minutes, until golden brown. Remove from the oven and brush with the melted butter. Transfer to a wire rack to cool slightly. Serve warm.

Makes one 9-inch pie

1 recipe Plain Pie Pastry or Vinegar Pie Crust, unbaked (page 145)

1½ cups sugar

¼ cup all-purpose flour

¼ teaspoon salt

¼ teaspoon grated nutmeg

3 cups diced rhubarb stems

1 cup sliced strawberries

2 tablespoons unsalted butter, cut into small pieces

2 tablespoons unsalted butter, melted

Southern Pecan Pie

This pie is deep brown, dense, and chewy, not to mention so sweet that it will make your teeth ache.

✳ Preheat the oven to 350°F. Line a 9-inch pie plate with the dough and crimp the edges.

✳ In a large bowl, combine the butter, corn syrup, eggs, vanilla, salt, and sugar and stir until well mixed. Stir in the pecans. Pour the filling into the crust.

✳ Bake for about 45 minutes, until a thin knife inserted into the filling halfway between the crust and the center comes out clean. Transfer to a wire rack to cool. Serve at room temperature or chilled.

Makes one 9-inch pie

½ recipe Plain Pie Pastry or Vinegar Pie Crust, unbaked (page 145)

3 tablespoons unsalted butter, melted

½ cup light corn syrup

3 eggs, lightly beaten

1 teaspoon pure vanilla extract

Pinch of salt

1 cup sugar

1 cup pecans

Chapter 8

Cakes

Growing Pains

"All old men love pound cake."

—Mildred Rowe

One of Mildred's spots in the restaurant was the corner stool at what is left of the original counter. She would perch there, chat with the customers, watch food as it came out of the kitchen, glance around the floor, and look at tables that needed clearing, cups that needed filling, or customers who did not look happy. Her personal agenda was to make sure people forgot their problems when they came to the restaurant. Sometimes, she would get on a person's nerves—until she saw them smiling.

Sitting on her stool, or on the English sleeping bench at the entryway, Mildred was often the picture of a sweet but wisecracking, Southern granny. As she moved about the place, taking care of customers, dropping into the kitchen to check on things, customers and employees felt like they knew her, like they were a part of the family.

Her barn-red restaurant now sits on Rowe Road. With its warm paneling and pleasant coloring, the restau-

The restaurant after the major renovation in 1986.

rant has the feel of a Virginia home. It is a carefully constructed image. From Mildred's days in Goshen, she felt that people wanted to feel at home while they were dining.

Many of Mildred employees were her best friends. Here is a group of women friends and employees gathered at Tootie's house. Tootie McLear is kneeling in front. Seated next to Mildred are Sheila Turner, Geneva Hamilton, and Sue Hilt.

Mildred's public persona was also carefully constructed. That she was a smart, sassy, down-home country woman was true. That she was a grandmother who loved to help customers with their babies and treat the little ones was also true. But she was more complicated than that.

In some ways, Mildred's business success in Staunton was imposed by others, though her food philosophies were certainly the backbone the restaurant's popularity. It was Willard and later her grown children, who insisted on expansion. Mildred wanted to include her children in the business decisions, but often found that she was outnumbered.

Brenda and Michael had formed a different business philosophy—they saw expansion and growth as positive forces. For example, against her wishes, they purchased several properties along the Route 250 corridor. One was a shopping center, another a hotel. But still, they saw numerous opportunities pass by because of Mildred's conservatism. They wanted to purchase even more properties along

"When our oldest daughter was just a baby, we visited the restaurant one Sunday and were greeted by Mrs. Rowe. She said, 'Bring that baby in here so she can have some real mashed potatoes instead of the kind out of the box.'"

—CAROLE HINTON, STAUNTON RESIDENT

A view of Mrs. Rowe's Restaurant today.

250—one of which would become the site of the present-day Cracker Barrel. Mildred would not hear of it.

"Why not?" Brenda and Michael wanted to know. They now had the money and the growth of the corridor seemed inevitable. "That's bad ground up there," she said. "I tried to plant beans there and they wouldn't grow. It's all rock." Sure enough, years later, when Cracker Barrel purchased the land and began excavating, the cost was enormous—because of the rock.

The next major step for the business was in 1986. Michael and Brenda, working together now, expanded the kitchen. They wanted to add another dining room as well. Mildred did not want to see it happen. Once again, it was her "if it ain't broke, don't fix it" attitude. But the new dining room gave the business seventy-five more seats and the staff doubled. Mildred, of course, rose to the new challenge.

This renovation proved hard to manage—it was difficult to keep serving customers while building a new kitchen. Daily catastrophes occurred, like the time the Lions Club was meeting there for breakfast.

A new sprinkler system had been installed in the kitchen, along with new grills and stoves and a new ventilation system. On this first day of operating the new equipment, something went wrong. The sprinkler system went off, spraying blue chemicals all over the food, the kitchen, and the staff.

Michael found himself telling a room full of Lions Club members that they would not be getting any breakfast that morning. "It was really a tough time. We couldn't keep the staff and we were having problems getting food out of the kitchen. Longtime customers were getting frustrated. After four or five months, though, it worked out," he says.

Having learned from the 1986 renovation, the next one went smoother. In 2000, the Rowes built a new entrance and waiting area that looks like an enclosed front porch, which adds to the welcoming ambience.

Mildred loved to travel, though she did not do much of it. She did go to Europe; this is a shot of her in Amsterdam. She also took her oldest grandchild, Sarah, to Alaska. She had announced that she would take every one of her grandchildren on a special trip, but Sarah turned out to be the only one.

As her adult children began to be more involved in the business, Mildred still came in every day to taste test, keep an eye on everything, and greet and chat with the customers. She also started to relax and enjoy life. She began to play golf at age sixty. It must have been stirring within her for years because when she was ready to take up the sport, it became her life. Her golf instructor said that if she had started at a young age, she could have been a pro.

Mildred was well known at the Ingleside Golf Club, not just for her golfing, but also for her food. She golfed frequently with Barb Sawyer, who said that Mildred brought baskets heaped with goodies with her to the golf course. Longtime customer and local realtor Don Sheets remembers Mildred telling him about picking blackberries on the golf course. "I think they are a little upset with me," she told him sheepishly one day. "I stopped at the sixth hole and picked about three quarts of blackberries."

Mildred's eccentricities extended into the business community—both with those she did business with and those that were her competition. One of those rival places was the Beverly Restaurant in Staunton, which is almost as old as Rowe's but has not expanded over the years. Mildred and Beverly's owners, Janet and Paul Thomas, took part in a little friendly banter from time to time. Mildred would often joke that Janet stole her recipes. "Well, maybe she stole mine," Janet said and laughed.

Willard was related to Paul, who was famous for his pie. Mildred often asked him, while sitting in his restaurant, if he wanted to come and work for her—and bring his pies with him.

Mildred's favorite local restaurant was Ever's Country Buffet in Mount Crawford, Virginia. It had a decidedly Mennonite influence. Owner Rudolph Ever began his restaurant career with the Buckhorn Inn and Mildred had helped him a lot. "Until then, I had only catered and I never had a restaurant before and Mildred gave me a lot of advice," he said. Incidentally, the Rowe-DiGrassie family has recently purchased Ever's from Rudolph.

Even though Mildred never wanted to see another "Mrs. Rowe's" restaurant, she probably would have agreed to the Ever's purchase. She was so fond of the place and the family. And if Michael wanted to do it, she would have supported it. She had come to trust his judgment above anyone else's.

Being the only boy in the family worked out well for Michael DiGrassie. He was Mildred's "favorite son" and she made no bones about it. Now Mildred's favorite son owns and operates her life's work—although other family members have taken their turns and contributed to its success.

Michael loves the challenge of the business and is ebullient when talking about the restaurant: what makes it different, how it offers benefits to the employees, how it is able to get better prices on some food because of its aggressive bidding techniques. He loves to tell the story of the restaurant and the story of his mother's life.

He inherited his mother's exactness for figures and business. If Mildred had been born later, with a different set of circumstances, she may have been an engineer—given the sharp, meticulous way her mind worked.

Michael still keeps up his engineer's license, even though he has not worked in that capacity since 1990. He volunteers his engineering expertise at a local construction company and has used his skills to build a home and to advise friends and family on the building of their homes. Whether they take or want that advice, though, is another matter.

In this regard, he is exactly like his mother.

Aunt Sissy's Chocolate Cake

Aunt Sissy is what Mildred's children called her sister Estelle. The children often gathered in Estelle's kitchen in hopes of persuading her to make this cake.

✳ Preheat the oven to 350°F. Grease and flour two 9-inch cake pans.

✳ Combine the butter and sugar in a large bowl and beat with an electric mixer until light and fluffy. One at a time, add the eggs, beating well after each addition. Mix in the chocolate. Sift the flour and baking powder together into another bowl. Add the flour mixture alternately with the milk to the chocolate mixture, beginning and ending with the dry ingredients. Stir in the vanilla. Pour the batter into the prepared pans and bake for 25 minutes, until a knife or toothpick inserted into the center comes out clean. Remove the cakes from the oven and allow to cool in the pans on a wire rack for 10 minutes. Turn the cakes out onto the rack and cool completely.

✳ To make the icing, melt the butter and chocolate in the top of a double boiler set over simmering water. Remove from the heat and stir in the sugar, egg, salt, and vanilla. Beat, using an electric mixer on medium, until the icing is creamy.

✳ Place 1 of the cake layers on a plate and spread the top with the icing. Place the other layer on top. Frost the top and sides of the cake with the icing, covering evenly.

Makes one 9-inch layer cake

½ cup unsalted butter, at room temperature

2 cups granulated sugar

2 eggs

4 ounces unsweetened chocolate, melted and cooled

2 cups cake flour

2 teaspoons baking powder

1½ cups milk

2 teaspoons pure vanilla extract

Aunt Sissy's Chocolate Icing

½ cup unsalted butter

2 ounces unsweetened chocolate

1½ cups confectioners' sugar

1 egg, lightly beaten

Pinch of salt

1 teaspoon pure vanilla extract

Estelle's son Parker Jr. and his cousin Linda DiGrassie after eating Estelle's famous chocolate cake. Mildred used to babysit Parker Jr. He is the person who first called Mildred "Moo-Moo," which became her nickname from that point on.

Best-Ever Pound Cake

Pound cake can be traced to England in the 1700s. It originally contained one pound each of butter, sugar, eggs, and flour. No leaveners were used other than the air whipped into the batter. In the days when many people couldn't read, this simple convention made it simple to remember recipes. Seven recipes for pound cakes can be found between Mildred's handwritten cookbook and the restaurant's cookbook. Mildred was a great observer of what people ate at parties. She noted that all of the old men went for the pound cake.

Makes one 10-inch tube cake

1½ cups unsalted butter, at room temperature

½ cup vegetable shortening

3 cups sugar

6 eggs

4 cups all-purpose flour

1 cup milk

1 teaspoon pure vanilla extract

1 teaspoon pure lemon extract

✳ Preheat the oven to 325°F and place a rack in the center position. Grease and flour a 10-inch tube pan.

✳ Combine the butter and shortening in a bowl and beat, using an electric mixer at medium speed, for about 2 minutes, until soft and creamy. Gradually add the sugar and continue to beat at medium speed for 5 to 7 minutes, until the mixture is fluffy. One at a time, add the eggs, beating just until the yellow disappears; do not overmix. Add the flour alternately with the milk, beating at low speed and beginning and ending with the flour. Mix just until blended after each addition. Scrape down the bottom and sides of the bowl several times with a rubber spatula to uniformly mix the batter. Stir in the vanilla and lemon extract.

✳ Spoon the batter into the prepared cake pan and smooth the top. Bake for 1½ hours, until a tester inserted into the center comes out clean. Transfer to a wire rack and allow to cool in the pan for 15 minutes. Run a knife around the sides to completely loosen and invert the cake onto the rack. Invert onto another wire rack so that the rounded top is up and the flat bottom is down. Allow to cool completely.

✳ Serve at once, store at room temperature in an airtight container, or cover with plastic wrap and aluminum foil and freeze for up to 2 months. If frozen, thaw before unwrapping.

Black Walnut–Apple Pound Cake

This cake recipe was found written in one of Mildred's cookbooks. Black walnuts grow freely in the Appalachians, though harvesting them can be a complicated ritual. They are never plucked from the tree. After they fall and become brown, the nut is almost ready. It is best to leave the skin on and let the nuts dry out a bit before peeling it off. To hull her walnuts, Mildred would spread them out in the driveway and let cars roll over them. The black walnut's flavor is more pungent than the English walnut's, but it is difficult to find out of season. Mrs. Garrison used to bring black walnuts into the restaurant and sell them to the customers and to Mildred, who always kept a bagful in her freezer for a winter treat. Mrs. Garrison used her walnut money for her Christmas fund.

✳ Preheat the oven to 325°F. Grease and flour a 10-inch tube or Bundt pan.

✳ In a large bowl, combine the sugar, oil, and eggs and mix using an electric mixer. In a separate bowl, combine the flour, baking soda, cinnamon, and nutmeg. Add the dry ingredients to the egg mixture and mix well. Mix in the vanilla. Add the apples and walnuts and fold in with a rubber spatula.

✳ Scrape the batter into the prepared pan and bake for about 1 hour and 15 minutes, until a tester inserted into the center comes out clean. Transfer to a wire rack and allow to cool in the pan for 20 minutes. Turn the cake out onto the rack and allow to cool completely.

Makes one 10-inch cake

2 cups sugar

1½ cups vegetable oil

3 eggs

3 cups all-purpose flour

2 teaspoons baking soda

1½ teaspoons ground cinnamon

1 teaspoon ground nutmeg

2 teaspoon pure vanilla extract

3 cups peeled and finely diced York apples (about 4 apples)

2 cups chopped black walnuts or English walnuts

Blackberry Jam Cake with Caramel Icing

The original recipe used fresh blackberries. Michael did not care for the seeds, so now the restaurant uses seedless blackberry jam.

✳ Preheat the oven to 350°F. Grease and flour a 10-inch tube pan, a 10-inch Bundt pan, or three 9-inch cake pans.

✳ Place the egg whites in a bowl and beat to stiff peaks using an electric mixer.

✳ In a separate large bowl, combine the butter and sugar and beat, using an electric mixer, until light and fluffy. Mix in the egg yolks, jam, and vanilla. In another bowl, stir together the flour, baking soda, baking powder, salt, cloves, cinnamon, and nutmeg. Add the flour mixture alternately with the buttermilk to the jam mixture, beginning and ending with the dry ingredients. Add the egg whites and fold in with a rubber spatula. Fold in the nuts.

✳ Scrape the batter into the prepared pan and bake until a tester inserted into the center comes out clean, 20 to 25 minutes for the layers and 60 to 80 minutes for a 10-inch cake. Remove the cake from the oven and allow to cool in the pan on a wire rack for 20 minutes. Turn the cake out onto the rack and cool completely.

✳ To make the icing, melt the butter in a large saucepan over low heat. Stir in the brown sugar and cook, stirring constantly, for 2 minutes, until the sugar dissolves. Add the milk and stir until smooth. Remove from the heat and with an electric mixer on medium, beat in enough confectioners' sugar to make the icing thick enough to spread.

✳ Frost the top and sides of the cake with the caramel icing. (If making a layer cake, use the icing between the layers and on the top and sides.)

Makes one 10-inch cake
or one 9-inch layer cake

3 eggs, separated

⅔ cup unsalted butter, at room temperature

1½ cups granulated sugar

1 cup seedless blackberry jam

1 teaspoon pure vanilla extract

3 cups all-purpose flour

1 teaspoon baking soda

2 teaspoons baking powder

½ teaspoon salt

½ teaspoon ground cloves

½ teaspoon ground cinnamon

½ teaspoon ground nutmeg

1 cup buttermilk

1 cup chopped black walnuts

Caramel Icing

⅓ cup unsalted butter

1 cup packed brown sugar

⅓ cup milk

2½ to 3 cups confectioners' sugar, sifted

Brownstone Front Cake

"Very old recipe" is scribbled next to this recipe in Mildred's handwritten cookbook. Brownstone Front Cake is often described as old-fashioned or Southern. The name may derive from the fact that the icing has a similar color to brownstone building facades. Since it needs to be mixed and baked just right, this recipe is for an experienced baker. The key is maintaining the right amount of moisture. The memory of this cake, the "most moist cake I have ever eaten," keeps Aaron trying to perfect the recipe at the restaurant today.

✳ Preheat the oven to 350°F. Grease and flour two 10-inch cake pans.

✳ In a bowl, combine the cocoa powder and baking soda. Pour the boiling water over the cocoa mixture. Mix thoroughly and set aside.

✳ Place the butter in a bowl and beat, using an electric mixer, until creamy and smooth. Add the sugar and continue to blend. One at a time, add the eggs, beating well after each addition. Add the flour alternately with the buttermilk and mix until incorporated. Just prior to baking, stir in the cocoa mixture. Divide the batter evenly between the pans and bake for 12 to 15 minutes, until a tester inserted into the center comes out clean. Remove the cakes from the oven and allow to cool in the pan on a wire rack for 20 minutes. Turn the cakes out onto the rack and cool completely.

✳ To make the icing, in a deep saucepan, combine the brown sugar, granulated sugar, and the ½ cup milk over medium heat. Cook for about 20 minutes, until the mixture forms a soft ball when dropped into cold water. Add the butter and vanilla and stir until melted. Remove from the heat and beat until it starts to get firm. Add the confectioners' sugar and the 2 tablespoons milk and stir to mix. Allow to cool.

✳ Place 1 of the cake layers on a plate and spread the top with the icing. Place the other layer on top. Frost the top and sides of the cake with the icing, covering evenly.

Makes one 10-inch layer cake

¾ cup cocoa powder

2 teaspoons baking soda

1 cup boiling water

1 cup unsalted butter, at room temperature

3 cups granulated sugar

4 eggs

4 cups all-purpose flour, sifted

1 cup buttermilk

Caramel Icing

1½ cups packed dark brown sugar

½ cup granulated sugar

½ cup plus 2 tablespoons milk

4 tablespoons unsalted butter

1 teaspoon pure vanilla extract

½ cup confectioners' sugar

Brown Sugar Pound Cake

Finding the source for recipes can sometimes be difficult because people change them often and good ones find their way around quickly. In Bertha's handwritten notebook, Mildred is listed as the source for this recipe and a date is actually given: February 12, 1966. So, it's very possible that this cake is an original.

✳ Preheat the oven to 300°F. Grease and flour a 10-inch tube pan or Bundt pan.

✳ In a large bowl, combine the butter and shortening and beat, using an electric mixer, until creamy. Add the brown and granulated sugars and beat until light and fluffy. One at a time, add the eggs, beating well after each addition. In a separate bowl, stir together the flour, baking powder, and salt. Add the flour mixture alternately with the milk to the sugar mixture, beginning and ending with the dry ingredients. Mix in the vanilla. Dust the nuts with flour and fold into the batter with a rubber spatula.

✳ Scrape the batter into the prepared cake pan and bake for 45 to 55 minutes, until a tester inserted into the center comes out clean. Transfer to a wire rack and allow to cool in the pan for 20 minutes. Turn the cake out onto the rack and cool completely.

Makes one 10-inch cake

1 cup unsalted butter, at room temperature

½ cup vegetable shortening

1 pound brown sugar (2½ packed cups)

1 cup granulated sugar

5 eggs

3 cups all-purpose flour

1 teaspoon baking powder

Pinch of salt

1 cup milk

1 teaspoon pure vanilla extract

1 cup chopped black walnuts

Cranberry Cake

A festive cake, great for the holidays. Pearl, one of Mildred's sisters, wrote this recipe. The orange zest plays off of the tangy cranberries for depth of fruit flavor.

✳ Preheat the oven to 325°F. Grease and flour a 10-inch tube pan.

✳ Sift the flour into a large bowl and then sift it again with the sugar, salt, baking soda, and baking powder. Stir in the dates, nuts, cranberries, and orange zest. In a separate bowl, stir together the eggs, buttermilk, and oil. Stir the egg mixture into the flour mixture and mix well.

✳ Pour the batter into the prepared pan and bake for 55 to 60 minutes, until a knife or toothpick inserted into the center comes out clean.

✳ To make the glaze, combine the juice and sugar in a saucepan over medium-high heat. Bring to a simmer and stir for 2 minutes, until the sugar dissolves. Do not boil. Use at once or keep warm over low heat.

✳ Remove the cake from the oven and pour the warm glaze over it. Let cool in the pan on a wire rack for 30 minutes. Turn the cake out onto the rack and let sit for 24 hours at room temperature before serving.

Makes one 10-inch cake

2½ cups all-purpose flour

1 cup sugar

1 teaspoon salt

1 teaspoon baking soda

1 teaspoon baking powder

1 cup diced pitted dates

1 cup chopped black walnuts or pecans

1 cup whole fresh or thawed cranberries

Grated zest of 2 oranges

2 eggs, lightly beaten

1 cup buttermilk

¾ cup vegetable oil

Orange Glaze

¾ cup freshly squeezed orange juice

¾ cup sugar

Fresh Apple Cake with Caramel Sauce

Carroll Mays, Bertha's son, penned this versatile recipe. You can leave out the nuts or raisins and the cake will still be packed with spicy, warm, hearty flavors. Wrapped in a cheesecloth, this cake will keep moist in the refrigerator for up to six months.

✳ Preheat the oven to 350°F. Grease and flour a 9 by 13-inch baking dish.

✳ In a bowl, combine the oil, sugar, and eggs and stir well. Sift the flour, baking soda, and cinnamon together into the egg mixture. Stir in the vanilla, apples, coconut, nuts, and raisins.

✳ Pour the batter into the prepared dish. Bake for 50 minutes, until a tester inserted into the center comes out clean.

✳ To make the sauce, combine the butter, milk, and sugar in a saucepan over medium heat. Bring to a boil and keep hot. The consistency will remain thin.

✳ Remove the cake from the oven and pour the hot sauce over it. Transfer the cake in the pan to a wire rack and allow to cool. Cut into squares to serve.

Makes one 9 by 13-inch cake

1½ cups vegetable oil

2 cups granulated sugar

2 eggs

2 cups all-purpose flour

1 teaspoon baking soda

1 teaspoon ground cinnamon

2 teaspoons pure vanilla extract

3 cups peeled, cored, and grated York apples (about 4 apples)

1 cup sweetened flaked coconut

1 cup chopped black walnuts

1 cup raisins

Caramel Sauce

4 tablespoons unsalted butter

2 tablespoons milk

½ cup plus 1 tablespoon confectioners' sugar

Mildred's Fresh Coconut Cake

Coconut was one of the tropical flavors that Mildred loved. This is the cake that her children could not enjoy Christmas without. The lemon extract gives it an extra fruity depth. Michael notes that this cake is better if placed in an airtight container in the freezer for a day or two before serving.

✳ To make the icing, combine the egg whites, sugar, water, corn syrup, and cream of tartar in the top of a double boiler set over boiling water. Whisk until well combined. Bring to a boil and cook, whisking constantly, for 7 minutes, until stiff peaks form. Remove from the heat and stir in the coconut. Let cool to room temperature before icing the cake.

✳ Preheat the oven to 325°F. Grease and flour two 9-inch cake pans.

✳ Combine the butter and sugar in a large bowl and beat, using an electric mixer, until light and fluffy. One at time, add the eggs, beating well after each addition. In a separate bowl, stir together the flour and baking powder. Add the flour mixture alternately with the milk to the butter mixture, beginning and ending with the dry ingredients. Stir in the vanilla and lemon extract.

✳ Divide the batter between the prepared pans and bake for 25 to 30 minutes, until they spring back when gently pressed on top and a tester inserted into the center comes out clean. Transfer the cakes to a wire rack and allow to cool for 10 minutes. Turn the cakes out onto the rack and cool completely.

✳ Cut the layers in half horizontally with a serrated knife to make 4 layers. Place 1 layer on a plate and spread the top with the icing. Carefully place another layer on top of the first and spread the top with the icing. Repeat with the 2 remaining layers and then frost the top and sides of the cake. Refrigerate until chilled before serving. Store refrigerated.

Makes one 9-inch layer cake

Icing

2 egg whites

1½ cups sugar

⅓ cup water

1 tablespoon light corn syrup

¼ teaspoon cream of tartar

2 cups fresh unsweetened grated coconut or fresh frozen unsweetened coconut, thawed

1 cup unsalted butter, at room temperature

2 cups sugar

6 eggs

3 cups all-purpose flour

1 teaspoon baking powder

1 cup milk

1 teaspoon pure vanilla extract

1 teaspoon pure lemon extract

Hot Applesauce Cake

Apples, of course, were a mainstay for Mildred all of her life. Her father had an orchard and one of Virginia's biggest crops is apples. Mildred was constantly fiddling with apple dishes, including making and canning her own applesauce from Summer Rambo apples. She probably used homemade applesauce in this cake.

Makes one 9 by 13-inch cake

1 cup unsalted butter, at room
    temperature

2 cups sugar

2 eggs

3½ cups all-purpose flour

2 teaspoons baking soda

½ teaspoon salt

2 teaspoons ground cinnamon

1 teaspoon ground cloves

½ teaspoon ground nutmeg

½ teaspoon ground mace

2 cups raisins

1 cup chopped black walnuts

2 cups applesauce

* Preheat the oven to 325°F. Grease and flour a tube cake pan.

* Combine the butter and sugar in a large bowl and beat, using an electric mixer, until light and fluffy. One at a time, add the eggs, beating well after each addition. In a separate bowl, stir together the flour, baking soda, salt, cinnamon, cloves, nutmeg, and mace. Add the flour mixture to the butter mixture, mixing until the batter is just combined. Dust the raisins and nuts with flour and fold them into the batter with a rubber spatula.

* Heat the applesauce in a small saucepan over medium heat. Stir the hot applesauce into the batter.

* Pour the batter into the prepared pan and bake for 55 to 60 minutes, until a tester inserted into the center comes out clean.

* Transfer the cake in the pan to a wire rack and allow to cool for 20 minutes. Turn the cake out onto the rack and cool completely.

A slice of Fresh Coconut Cake.

Mandarin Orange Cake

Dolly, Mildred's niece, gave her this recipe. She remembers that when she was a child her Aunt Millie bought her patent leather shoes one year and dressed her up like Shirley Temple—one of Mildred's favorite performers at the time. "We walked around the streets of Covington. She made such a fuss. I just will never forget it," says Dolly. Mildred asked for this recipe for years and finally got it when she visited Rich Patch for the last time.

* Preheat the oven to 350°F. Grease and flour two 9-inch cake pans.

* Combine the eggs, oil, and sugar in a bowl and beat, using an electric mixer, until well blended. Add the cake mix and beat for about 2 minutes, until the batter is smooth. Stir in the oranges.

* Divide the batter between the prepared pans and bake for about 25 minutes, until the tops spring back when gently pressed and a tester inserted into the center comes out clean. Remove the cakes from the oven and allow to cool in the pans on a wire rack for 10 minutes. Turn the cakes out onto the rack and cool completely.

* To make the topping, combine the pudding mix and whipped topping in a bowl and stir until smooth. Fold in the pineapple.

* Place 1 of the cake layers on a plate and spread the top with the topping. Place the second layer on top of the first and frost the top and sides of the cake. Refrigerate until chilled before serving. Store refrigerated.

Makes one 9-inch layer cake

4 eggs

¾ cup vegetable oil

½ cup sugar

1 (18.25-ounce) box yellow cake mix

1 (15-ounce) can mandarin oranges, drained

Pineapple Topping

1 (5.1-ounce) box instant vanilla pudding mix

1 (8-ounce) container nondairy whipped topping, thawed

1 (15.25-ounce) can crushed pineapple, drained

Pineapple Pound Cake

Crushed pineapple, considered a treat at one time in the mountains, gives this cake a different, more crumbly texture than most pound cakes. You might need to slice it with a serrated knife for a clean cut. For extra flavor, top with pecans or cinnamon ice cream.

✳ Preheat the oven to 325°F. Grease and flour a 10-inch tube pan or Bundt pan.

✳ Combine the shortening, butter, and sugar in a large bowl and beat, using an electric mixer, until light and fluffy. One at a time, add the eggs, beating well after each addition. In a separate bowl, stir together the flour and baking powder. Add the flour mixture alternately with the milk to the butter mixture, beginning and ending with the dry ingredients. Stir in the vanilla. Add the pineapple and juice and fold in with a rubber spatula.

✳ Scrape the batter into the prepared pan and bake for about 90 minutes, until a tester inserted into the center comes out clean.

✳ To make the glaze, combine all of the ingredients in a saucepan over medium-high heat. Bring to a simmer, stirring, for 2 minutes, until the sugar dissolves. Use at once or keep warm over low heat.

✳ Remove the cake from the oven and allow to cool in the pan on a wire rack for 10 minutes. Turn the cake out onto a plate and pour the hot glaze over the top. Allow to cool completely before serving.

Makes one 10-inch cake

½ cup vegetable shortening

1 cup unsalted butter, at room temperature

2 cups granulated sugar

6 eggs

3 cups sifted all-purpose flour

1 teaspoon baking powder

¼ cup milk

1 teaspoon pure vanilla extract

¾ cup canned crushed pineapple, undrained

Pineapple Glaze

4 tablespoons unsalted butter

1½ cups confectioners' sugar

1 cup canned crushed pineapple, well drained

Prune Cake

This cake is surprisingly delicious and extremely moist. The prunes don't actually impart a prune flavor, but give the cake lots of body.

✳ Preheat the oven to 300°F. Grease and flour a 9 by 13-inch baking dish.

✳ Place the prunes in a small saucepan and add just enough water to cover them. Bring to a simmer over medium heat. Cover and cook until the prunes are completely soft, 20 to 30 minutes. Add more water if the mixture becomes too dry and begins to stick to the sides of the pan. Drain and mash the prunes with a fork.

✳ Combine the oil and sugar in a large bowl and mix using an electric mixer. Add the eggs and mix well. In a separate bowl, stir together the flour, baking soda, salt, cinnamon, nutmeg, and allspice. Add the flour mixture alternately with the buttermilk to the sugar mixture, beginning and ending with the dry ingredients. Add the pecans and prunes and fold in with a rubber spatula.

✳ Pour the batter into the prepared pan and bake for 60 to 65 minutes, until a tester inserted into the center comes out clean.

✳ To make the icing, combine all of the ingredients in a large, deep saucepan over medium-high heat. Stir well and bring to a vigorous boil. Stir occasionally with a long-handled spoon for about 15 minutes, until the mixture forms a soft ball when dropped into cold water. Use at once.

✳ Remove the cake from the oven and pour the hot icing over it. Transfer the cake in the pan to a wire rack and allow to cool completely before serving.

Makes one 9 by 13-inch cake

1 cup pitted prunes

1 cup vegetable oil

1½ cups sugar

3 eggs

2 cups all-purpose flour

1 teaspoon baking soda

½ teaspoon salt

1 teaspoon ground cinnamon

1 teaspoon ground nutmeg

1 teaspoon ground allspice

1 cup buttermilk

1 cup chopped pecans

Buttermilk Icing

1 cup sugar

4 tablespoons unsalted butter

½ teaspoon pure vanilla extract

½ teaspoon baking soda

½ cup buttermilk

Vanilla Wafer Cake

Virginia, Mildred's sister, came up with this recipe. Scratched next to it in a handwritten recipe book are the words rich *and* heavy. *Evidently, it is not a dessert for the lighthearted.*

✳ Preheat the oven to 325°F. Grease and flour a 10-inch tube pan or Bundt pan.

✳ Using an electric coffee grinder, finely grind the pecans.

✳ Combine the sugar and butter in a large bowl and beat, using an electric mixer, until light and fluffy. One at a time, add the eggs, beating well after each addition. Add the vanilla wafers alternately with the milk to the butter mixture, beginning and ending with the wafers. Add the coconut and pecans and fold in with a rubber spatula.

✳ Scrape the batter into the prepared pan and bake for 60 to 70 minutes, until a knife or toothpick inserted into the center comes out clean. Transfer the cake in the pan to a wire rack and allow to cool for 20 minutes. Turn the cake out onto the rack and cool completely before serving.

Makes one 10-inch cake

1½ cup pecans

1½ cups sugar

¾ cup unsalted butter, at room temperature

6 eggs

1 (12-ounce) box vanilla wafers, very finely crushed

½ cup milk

¾ cup plus 2 tablespoons sweetened flaked coconut

Chapter 9

Other Desserts

Ever After

"Eat dessert first, so you'll be sure to have room for it."

—Mildred Rowe

If you were to chart out Mildred's entire life, there would be highs and lows and shifts forward and backward, circular patterns folding into one another. In every person's life, there is at least one major turning point. For Mildred, it was her second marriage to Willard Rowe that shifted her life onto a different plane.

She was still faced with a lot of hard work and struggle, though the struggles took on a different texture and were softened by her success. As she tried to find her place beside Willard,

Moo-Moo's eleven grandchildren, gathered in 1991. Clockwise from top left, they are: Nicholas, Aaron, Anne, Wynne, Sarah, David, Stevan, Lesley, Jane, Kate, and Grey.

then without Willard, Mildred still carried her wounds, insecurities, and doubts. She did her best to keep them below the surface, but in later years, an emotional bubble or two would often erupt. This baffled her family and close friends. Mildred had been a vision of stalwart strength and steadfast security to them. They could not reconcile that person with the one who cried at the mention of Eugene DiGrassie's name or her Goshen restaurant. After all, that was so long ago.

She enjoyed her success and lavished herself, family, and friends with gifts. She loved her fur coat, had plenty of beautiful shoes, and always wore tasteful dresses. She took great pride in her appearance and in her lovely home. But none of those things

Mildred received fan letters from time to time. Some folks also loved taking their picture with her. This photo of Whitney Wilkins came with a note, "This is a picture of our granddaughter [with Mildred]. Every time we drive by Mrs. Rowe's, she wants to stop." Whitney had also written a note.

made her eyes sparkle as much as a perfectly baked pan of golden, creamy macaroni and cheese or a bucket full of fresh, deep purple, juicy blackberries.

Most people like to talk about themselves, which makes it easy to profile their personality. But Mildred did not like to talk about herself. This could have been her humbleness, fading memory, or an unwillingness to disturb thoughts and feelings that were buried long ago.

The day she traveled to her home place in 2002, Mildred talked about the landscape, the trees, and the flowers planted along the highway. She talked about how dry everything looked—that being a year of incredible drought. Into the quiet and humming of the wheels on the road, all of a sudden her voice would ring out, "Oh my, look at the view over there."

Here was a woman born and bred in these mountains, and she was still awed by their beauty. Here was a woman who could have anything she wanted. Yet that day, she was focused on a dilapidated Victorian writing desk at the Old Rock House, where her grandmother had lived. She thought she could fix it and take it home with her.

"That was my grandmother's desk and she'd hate to see the condition it's in," she said. "Why don't you go back in there and get it for me?" She asked several times.

Often when people speak of Mildred, they mention her tenacity and strong will. Some would even call her bossy. As hard as she tried, she could not possibly

Chocolate Macaroons

Mildred loved to pick on Rod Stoner, the director of food services at the Greenbrier, a top-notch West Virginia resort that boasts some of the finest dining in the country. He would often stop by the restaurant, and one day he asked Mildred if he could have her chocolate macaroon recipe.

"Ohh," she said. "I couldn't give that to you. That's a special recipe."

Several months later, he was at the Tamarack, an upscale arts and craft center in West Virginia. The Greenbrier provides their food service. He sampled the macaroons and lo and behold, it was the same recipe.

"Did you get these from Mrs. Rowe?" he asked the chef. "How did you get her to part with the recipe?

"She didn't sell these to us or give us the recipe, we bought them from a distributor," the chef explained.

Stoner knew he had been duped. When he confronted her, she laughed and laughed and said, "Well, I told you I couldn't give you the recipe!"

---

do everything herself, so maybe telling people what to do was her way of passing on wisdom.

Though Mildred was a pioneer in the restaurant field and she could be viewed as a feminist icon, she would not have considered herself a feminist. She worked as hard as any man, probably harder than two men combined, and she was successful. To her, the formula seemed pretty simple.

The main circle of Mildred's life began deep in the mountains, a place of hardship, but also wisdom and great beauty. While she was a wild-haired, green-eyed girl, Mildred roamed the hills and fields and soaked in every bit of it. She was not afraid of death, for she had seen it many times, and, like a good Baptist, she firmly believed in a heaven. But she was always more focused on this life and the living.

The extreme pleasure that she took in food was one example of her embrace of life. Another was her connection with people. And then there was her love of colorful, euphemistic language. She used to say things like "I've got my teeth set for fried chicken," "I'm as stuffed as a tick," or "I'm so hungry my big ones are eatin' my little ones." These expressions are prevalent in the Appalachians, and sometimes it's hard to figure out what they mean. Mildred delivered them with such verve and never stopped using them, unlike most other emigrants from the mountains, who left such language behind.

Her love of life extended into her business as she created a home away from home for both locals and tourists. Mrs. Rowe's Restaurant and Bakery has become a place where families gather for birthdays, local philanthropists meet to plan new hospitals, politicians assemble to strategize, and travelers find a haven from the road. All of these people move in and out of the restaurant, along with the locals who drop by for a meal and to check on the local gossip and latest events. Whether they know it or not, they have all been touched in some way by Mildred Rowe's vision of home and food and her welcoming table.

Mildred often said that life wouldn't be worth living without good food, most especially a little something sweet. She reveled in desserts. In a gracious way, she often persuaded her patrons to eat a little more by listing the desserts available for the day.

Dessert is a treat, but for little Mildred Craft growing up in the back country of the Appalachians, it was probably almost nonexistent. The timing would have to be perfect. If her mother happened to have a little extra flour, sugar, milk, and eggs at the exact time the apple or blackberry harvest was ripe, and if she had the time and energy to conjure up an apple pie or blackberry cobbler after doing a myriad of other daily chores, then Mildred might have gotten a taste of something sweet from her mother's woodstove.

Dessert, then, became an important, enjoyable part of Mildred's life. The day before she passed away, she indulged in several helpings of the restaurant's banana pudding.

Apple Brown Betty

Every Virginia family has their own favorite version of Apple Brown Betty; this versatile recipe will quickly become your own. In late summer and fall, Virginia roadside stands are full of some of the most flavorful apples. Virginians will tell you that they are better than any apple in the world. Serve the dessert warm with a scoop of real vanilla ice cream.

✳ Preheat the oven to 450°F. Butter a 9 by 13-inch baking dish.

✳ Combine the apples, granulated sugar, raisins, nutmeg, and cinnamon in a large, heavy pot over high heat. Bring to a boil. In a small bowl, stir together the cornstarch and water to make a smooth paste. Stir the cornstarch mixture into the apple mixture and decrease the heat to medium. Simmer for 5 minutes, until thickened. Pour into the prepared baking dish.

✳ In a bowl, combine the brown sugar, breadcrumbs, and butter and stir well. Sprinkle over the apple mixture. Bake for about 30 minutes, until golden brown. Serve warm.

Serves 8 to 10

4 pounds York or Stayman
 apples, peeled, cored, and
 sliced (about 8 cups), or
 3½ pounds canned apples

2 cups granulated sugar

½ cup raisins

1½ teaspoons ground nutmeg

1½ teaspoons ground cinnamon

5 teaspoons cornstarch

¼ cup water

¾ cup packed light brown sugar

3 cups finely ground fresh
 breadcrumbs

6 tablespoons unsalted butter,
 melted

Apple Dumplings

"I am the only one of the grandchildren that knows how to make apple dumplings. Moo-Moo showed me how," Wynne DiGrassie proudly announced during an interview. When this was mentioned to other family members, Brenda just responded that "Wynne may be the only grandchild who knows how to make them, but I certainly know how." Also, Aaron, Wynne's chef-brother, says he knows how to make them, but not as well as his sister. Evidently, the apple dumplings—and the passing on of Mildred's traditions—was an important acknowledgment in the family. Though the recipe is not secret, Mildred's technique is a difficult thing to master— without her personal supervision. This seasonal dish is only on the menu in the autumn. Topped with cinnamon or vanilla ice cream, and served in a mini bread loaf, it's hard to stop eating.

✳ Preheat the oven to 375°F. Butter a 9 by 9-inch baking dish.

✳ Combine the ⅔ cup sugar, ¼ teaspoon of the cinnamon, the 2 tablespoons butter, and the water in a small saucepan over medium-high heat. Bring to a boil and cook, stirring constantly, for 3 minutes, until the sauce is slightly thick, like the consistency of maple syrup. Remove from the heat.

✳ Sift the flour and salt together into a large bowl. Add the shortening and ice water. Mix by hand to make a soft dough. Do not knead the dough too much or it will be tough. Divide the dough into 4 equal pieces. Roll out each piece of dough into a ⅛-inch thick and ¼-inch wide square on a lightly floured surface.

✳ Place an apple in the center of each square of dough. In a small bowl, stir together the ½ cup sugar and remaining 1½ teaspoons cinnamon. Pour into the apple core holes. Lightly moisten the edges of the pastry with water and fold up the corners over the apples. Pinch the edges of the dough together to seal.

Serves 4

⅔ cup plus ½ cup sugar

1¾ teaspoons ground cinnamon

2 tablespoons plus 2 teaspoons unsalted butter

1½ cups water

2 cups all-purpose flour

1 teaspoon salt

¾ cup plus 2 tablespoons vegetable shortening

¼ cup ice water

4 large, tart apples, peeled and cored

✳ Pour 1 cup of the sauce in the bottom of the prepared baking dish. Stand the apples upright in the dish. Dot the top of each apple with ½ teaspoon of the remaining butter. Bake for 20 minutes. Remove the dish from the oven and pour the remaining sauce over the apples. Return to the oven and bake, basting with the sauce several times, for about 30 minutes, until golden brown. Serve warm.

"When Mother made apple dumplings, usually in the fall when apples are best, she made about two dozen or more at a time and shared them with anyone who happened to drop by. I've sampled a lot of apple dumplings, but none quite like hers. The secret is the perfect apple and her wonderful pastry."

—BRENDA HATHAWAY, MILDRED'S DAUGHTER

B. B.'s Fried Apple Butter Pies

Although these are called pies, they are actually more similar to turnovers.

✳ Combine the flour and salt in a large bowl. Cut in the shortening and butter with a pastry blender until the mixture is crumbly. Add enough of the milk to moisten the mixture. Press the dough together and divide into 8 pieces. On a lightly floured surface, roll out each piece of dough into a 4-inch round. Spread 2 heaping tablespoons of the apple butter in the center of each piece of dough. Fold the dough over to make a half-moon shape and crimp the edges with a fork.

✳ Over medium-low heat, melt equal amounts of shortening and butter to cover the bottom of a large skillet. Working in batches as necessary, add the pies and pan-fry, turning once, for 2 to 3 minutes, until golden brown on both sides. Transfer to paper towels to drain. Serve warm or at room temperature.

Serves 8

2 cups all-purpose flour

1 teaspoon salt

⅔ cup vegetable shortening, plus more for frying

4 tablespoons unsalted butter, plus more for frying

½ to ¾ cup milk

2 cups spiced apple butter

Virginia's Banana Pudding

Mildred's sister's flavor-packed 1950s take on a Southern classic. It's quicker and more convenient for the everyday cook. Instant vanilla pudding and whipped topping don't detract from the taste.

✳ In a large bowl, combine the pudding mix and milk and stir until smooth and thick. Stir in the sour cream and whipped topping.

✳ Layer the pudding mixture, bananas, and vanilla wafers in a large bowl, making at least 2 layers of each. Cover and refrigerate for at least 30 minutes, until well chilled. Serve cold.

Serves 8

2 large boxes instant vanilla pudding mix

3 cups whole milk, or 1 cup whole milk and 2 cups half-and-half

1 cup sour cream

1 (12-ounce) container nondairy whipped topping

7 bananas, sliced into ¼-inch-thick rounds

1 (12-ounce) box vanilla wafers

Banana Pudding

Vivian Obie, a cook and baker who worked at the restaurant for nearly forty years, is the source for this recipe. Many of Rowe's long-standing menu items come straight from her. Vivian is a proper lady, the kind who is shocked that young women go to church these days not wearing hose. She used to fuss at Mildred for speaking her mind so openly. "She'd put her hands on her hips and say whatever came to her mind," Vivian says.

Serves 6 to 8

Vivian Obie at her retirement party.

* Heat the milk in the top of a double boiler set over simmering water. In a small bowl, whisk together the egg yolks, cornstarch, sugar, and enough water to make a soupy paste. Whisk the egg yolk mixture into the warm milk. Cook, stirring constantly, for 15 minutes, until thickened to the consistency of pudding. Remove from the heat and stir in the vanilla and butter. Set side to cool slightly.

* Preheat the oven to 325°F. Cover the bottom of a 9 by 13-inch baking dish with half of the vanilla wafers. Slice the bananas into ½-inch-thick rounds and spread half of them over the wafers. (If slicing the bananas ahead of time, toss them with the lemon juice and water to prevent browning.) Cover the bananas with half of the pudding. Spread the remaining wafers over the pudding, followed by the remaining bananas. Pour the rest of the pudding over the top.

* Spread the meringue over the pudding and bake for 20 to 30 minutes, until browned. Serve warm, at room temperature, or chilled.

* Variation: Substitute coarsely crumbled vanilla wafers for the meringue. This version does not need to be baked.

4 cups milk

4 egg yolks

¼ cup cornstarch

¾ cup sugar

¼ to ½ cup water

2 teaspoons pure vanilla extract

4 teaspoons unsalted butter

1 (12-ounce) box vanilla wafers

3 to 4 firm bananas

2 tablespoons freshly squeezed lemon juice mixed with 1 tablespoon water (optional)

1 recipe Mrs. Rowe's Meringue (page 146)

*"**What a master work it is**: crunchy meringue wed to a bed of moist banana cake, its custard lumpy with bananas, this is the definitive banana pudding of the South—soothing food for grown-up babies; food that assures you that all is well with the world."*

—Jane and Michael Stern, from *Roadfood*

Blueberry Crisp with Old-Fashioned Lemon Sauce

Pretty much any fruit can be used in this dish. Serve it with lemon sauce or vanilla ice cream.

* Preheat the oven to 350°F. Butter an 8 by 8-inch baking dish.

* In a bowl, combine the brown sugar, breadcrumbs, and melted butter and stir well.

* Combine the blueberries, sugar, and the ¼ cup water in a large saucepan over medium-high heat. Bring to a boil, stirring for 2 minutes, until the sugar dissolves. In a small bowl, stir together the cornstarch and remaining ⅓ cup water to make a smooth paste. Gradually stir the cornstarch paste into the blueberry mixture and cook, stirring constantly, for 5 minutes, until thickened. Pour the blueberry mixture into the prepared baking dish. Sprinkle the brown sugar mixture over the filling. Bake the crisp for about 20 minutes, until browned and bubbly.

* To make the lemon sauce, in a large saucepan, combine the cornstarch, sugar, and the 2 cups water over medium-low heat. Stir well and bring to a simmer. Cook, stirring constantly, for 1 to 2 minutes, until very thick. Stir in the butter.

* In a small bowl, whisk together the egg yolk and remaining 1 tablespoon water. Stir into the sauce. Cook for 1 to 2 minutes, but do not let boil. Remove from the heat and stir in the lemon juice and lemon zest.

* Serve the crisp warm with the lemon sauce poured on top.

Serves 6 to 8

½ cup packed brown sugar

2 cups homemade soft breadcrumbs

4 tablespoons unsalted butter, melted

3 cups fresh or thawed blueberries

¾ cup granulated sugar

¼ cup plus ⅓ cup water

¼ cup cornstarch

Old-Fashioned Lemon Sauce

2 tablespoons cornstarch

½ cup sugar

2 cups plus 1 tablespoon cold water

2 tablespoons unsalted butter, at room temperature

1 egg yolk

3 tablespoons freshly squeezed lemon juice

1 teaspoon grated lemon zest

Boiled Custard

Linda Hanna, one of Mildred's daughters, remembers, "It wouldn't be Christmas without Mother's boiled custard and fresh coconut cake. I spent my first Christmas away from home in 1972. I was living in California and was faced with a sunny warm holiday without family or Mother's custard. I telephoned home for the recipe. Her first words were, 'Go out and buy a glass double boiler. It must be glass.' I scoured San Diego until I found one. I made the custard but it wasn't as good as hers. That was the first, last, and only Christmas away from home." The custard needs to be stirred constantly. Mildred's children would take turns stirring, perhaps for a chance to lick the creamy spoon.

✳ Heat the milk in a saucepan over medium-high heat. In a large bowl, whisk together the egg yolks, sugar, and salt. As soon as the milk begins to steam, gradually whisk it into the egg mixture.

✳ Pour the egg and milk mixture into the top of a double boiler set over gently simmering water. Cook, stirring constantly, for 20 minutes, until the custard is thick enough to coat the back of a spoon. Remove from the heat and stir in the vanilla.

✳ Transfer to individual dishes or a serving bowl and sprinkle the top with nutmeg. Refrigerate for at least 1 hour, until chilled and set up. Serve cold.

Serves 4 to 6

3 cups milk

4 egg yolks

¼ cup sugar

Pinch of salt

1 tablespoon pure vanilla extract

¼ teaspoon freshly grated nutmeg

Bread Pudding with Raisin Sauce

This is the restaurant's basic bread pudding recipe that is used as a starting point for others. Rowe's serves about fifteen varieties throughout the year—pumpkin, blackberry, chocolate, and so on. Save up your unused bread in a plastic bag in the freezer and use it for the breadcrumbs. This dessert is extremely home-friendly and is just as delicious without the raisin sauce. It's especially yummy served warm with milk and sugar sprinkled on it.

* Preheat the oven to 350°F. Butter a 9 by 13-inch baking dish. Spread the breadcrumbs in the bottom of the dish.

* In a bowl, combine the eggs, sugar, milk, and vanilla and stir until well blended. Pour over the bread and dust the top with the nutmeg. Bake for 55 to 65 minutes, until golden brown.

* To make the sauce, in a bowl, combine the raisins and 3 cups of the water and stir well. Set aside to soak for 30 to 60 minutes. Drain the raisins, reserving the water. In a large saucepan over medium-high heat, stir together the reserved soaking water, sugar, lemon juice, salt, butter, and nutmeg. Bring to a simmer, stirring for 2 minutes, until the sugar dissolves. In a small bowl, stir together the cornstarch and remaining ¼ cup water to make a smooth paste. Stir the cornstarch mixture into the saucepan and cook, stirring constantly, for 5 minutes, until thickened. Stir in the raisins and keep warm.

* Remove the bread pudding from the oven and brush the top with the melted butter. Serve warm with the raisin sauce poured over the pudding.

Serves 10 to 12

5 cups coarse fresh breadcrumbs

5 eggs

2 cups sugar

2 cups milk

2 teaspoons pure vanilla extract

½ teaspoon ground nutmeg

2 tablespoons unsalted butter, melted

Raisin Sauce

1 cup raisins

3¼ cups water

1 cup sugar

2 tablespoons freshly squeezed lemon juice

Pinch of salt

2 tablespoons unsalted butter

½ teaspoon ground nutmeg

3 tablespoons cornstarch

Pineapple Bread Pudding with Vanilla Custard Sauce

Bread pudding is an extremely versatile dish for the thrifty cook: It's a good way to use day-old bread and any fruit or flavoring you have on hand. This recipe combines Mildred's love of tropical flavors with her homespun thriftiness.

✴ Preheat the oven to 350°F. Butter a 9 by 13-inch baking dish.

✴ Spread the bread in the bottom of the dish. Drizzle the melted butter over the bread. Drizzle the reserved pineapple juice over the bread. Sprinkle the pineapple and raisins over the bread and mix lightly. In a bowl, combine the eggs, brown sugar, cinnamon, nutmeg, allspice, and milk and stir until well blended. Pour the egg mixture over the pineapple mixture.

✴ Bake for about 40 minutes, until the custard is set in the center of the pan.

✴ To make the sauce, place the milk in a double boiler over medium heat until hot but not boiling. In a small bowl, thoroughly combine the sugar, eggs, butter, cornstarch, and vanilla until smooth. Add the paste to the milk, stirring constantly, and cook until thickened, about 15 minutes. Pour over the custard and serve warm.

Serves 10 to 12

8 cups (1-inch) pieces day-old, firm white bread

½ cup unsalted butter, melted

2 cups crushed pineapple, drained with ½ cup juice reserved

1¼ cups raisins

3 eggs, lightly beaten

¾ cup packed brown sugar

¼ teaspoon ground cinnamon

¼ teaspoon ground nutmeg

⅛ teaspoon ground allspice

1 cups milk

Vanilla Custard Sauce

1½ cups milk

1 cup granulated sugar

3 eggs

1 tablespoon butter, melted

3 tablespoons cornstarch

1 teaspoon vanilla

Millionaire Pie

Mildred and Bertha made this dessert frequently and always called it Millionaire Pie, even though it is not technically a pie, nor does anyone know where the millionaire comes from. It has no crust, doesn't bake in a pie plate, and is really more of a cobbler. Mildred always would make it with peaches, blackberries, blueberries—whatever was in season.

✴ Preheat the oven to 400°F. Pour the melted butter into a 8 by 13-inch baking dish.

✴ In a bowl, combine the sugar, flour, milk, and baking powder and mix well. Pour into the baking dish. Sprinkle the fruit over the batter. Bake for about 30 minutes, until browned. Serve warm.

Serves 8

½ cup unsalted butter, melted

1 cup sugar

1 cup all-purpose flour

1 cup milk

2 teaspoons baking powder

2 cups peeled and diced fresh fruit, thawed fruit, canned fruit, or berries

Never-Fail Fudge

A convenient, easy recipe for folks that truly love fudge. Fudge is known as plate candy in some parts of the South.

✴ Butter a 9 by 13-inch baking dish.

✴ Combine the sugar and milk in a large, heavy pot over high heat. Bring to a rolling boil and cook, stirring constantly, for 7 minutes, until the mixture looks creamy and glossy. Remove from the heat and add the chocolate chips, butter, and marshmallow cream, stirring for 5 minutes, until melted, smooth, and well blended. Stir in the vanilla and nuts.

✴ Scrape into the prepared baking dish. Refrigerate for at least 30 minutes before cutting. Store covered and refrigerated.

Makes 5 pounds

4½ cups sugar

1 (8-ounce) can evaporated milk

3 (12-ounce) bags semisweet chocolate chips

½ cup unsalted butter

1 (8-ounce) jar marshmallow cream

1 tablespoon pure vanilla extract

1 cup chopped black walnuts

Oatmeal Raisin Cookies

Since you can't go wrong with this cookie, it's a good one to experiment with: leave out the raisins, add chocolate chips, or throw in some nuts. Walnuts particularly complement this cookie.

✳ Preheat the oven to 375°F. Lightly grease a baking sheet with butter-flavored vegetable shortening.

✳ Combine the shortening and sugar in a large bowl and beat, using an electric mixer, until light and fluffy. Add the eggs and molasses and mix well. Add the flour, oats, salt, cinnamon, and baking soda and stir with a wooden spoon until well mixed. Fold in the raisins.

✳ Drop the dough by rounded tablespoonfuls onto the prepared baking sheet. Bake for 10 to 12 minutes, until lightly browned. Transfer the cookies to a wire rack to cool.

Makes 4 dozen cookies

1 cup butter-flavored vegetable shortening

1 cup sugar

3 eggs

¼ cup molasses

2 cups all-purpose flour

2 cups quick-cooking rolled oats

½ teaspoon salt

½ teaspoon ground cinnamon

1 teaspoon baking soda

1½ cup raisins

Pecan-Chocolate Chunk Cookies

Every bite of these cookies is richer than the last. Peanuts can be substituted for the pecans for a saltier and less expensive version of this recipe.

* Preheat the oven to 375°F.

* In a large bowl, combine the butter, granulated sugar, and brown sugar and beat, using an electric mixer, until light and fluffy. Beat in the vanilla and eggs. In a separate bowl, stir together the flour, baking soda, and salt. Gradually add the flour mixture to the butter mixture and mix until incorporated. Fold in the chocolate and pecans.

* Drop the dough by rounded tablespoonfuls onto ungreased baking sheets. Bake for 9 to 10 minutes, until lightly browned. Transfer the cookies to a wire rack to cool.

Makes 6 dozen cookies

1 cup unsalted butter, at room temperature

¾ cup granulated sugar

¾ cup packed brown sugar

1 teaspoon pure vanilla extract

2 eggs

2¼ cups all-purpose flour

1 teaspoon baking soda

½ teaspoon salt

24 ounces semisweet chocolate baking chunks

1 cup coarsely chopped pecans

Pecan Puffs

Round balls of pastry, no bigger than a quarter, rolled in powdered sugar, offer a dry and crunchy nutty treat.

* Preheat the oven to 300°F.

* Using a electric coffee grinder, finely grind the pecans.

* In a large bowl, combine the butter and sugar and beat, using an electric mixer, until light and fluffy. Stir in the flour, pecans, and vanilla to make a stiff dough.

* One tablespoon at a time, form the dough into 24 balls and place them on a baking sheet. Bake for 40 minutes, until the exterior is very crispy.

* Remove the puffs from the oven and, while still hot, carefully toss them in the confectioners' sugar. Allow to cool and then toss them again in the confectioners' sugar. Serve at room temperature.

Makes 24 puffs

1½ cups pecans

½ cup unsalted butter, at room temperature

2 tablespoons granulated sugar

1 cup all-purpose flour

1 teaspoon pure vanilla extract

¾ cup confectioners' sugar

Epilogue

Gone, but Not Forgotten

Even on a snowy February day, Mrs. Rowe's Restaurant and Bakery is brimming with warmth and activity at 5:30 A.M. The business has its own time cycle and this is not considered early.

The bakers get to work first. Ken and Cynthia arrive around 2:00 A.M. and begin preparing pies, bread, muffins, and sometimes bread pudding or cobblers. So when the rest of the morning crew arrives, anywhere between 5:30 and 8:00 A.M., depending on their station, the air is filled with a myriad of luscious scents: bread, cinnamon, sometimes blackberry, sometimes apple.

Rowe's makes about fifty pies a day and thirty-five loaves of bread. The bread is so moist that it must be served the day after baking, otherwise it would fall apart. While bread is pulled out of the oven, luscious, gleaming chocolate filling is spooned enticingly into pies, as are dollops of golden, creamy coconut filling. Meringue grows like sugary clouds in the mixer. Artfully prepared cinnamon rolls, with sweet, white icing dripping off their edges, sit on trays lined with waxed paper.

Even though it is not yet 7:00 A.M., the salad lady is already in the kitchen, chopping away. Along with the breakfast grill chef, two people are prepping for lunch. Penny is fixing turkeys and making lasagna. Later, Aaron DiGrassie will coat about twenty half chickens and place them in a huge fryer filled with grease. While they are prepping for lunch, the breakfast station is center stage.

Homemade creamy-yellow buttermilk pancake batter sits in huge metal bowls ready to be ladled onto the griddle. Lightly browned puffs of buttermilk biscuits are bathed in gravy. The sound of eggs cracking and their greasy splat onto the hot grills fills the air. Plates seem to be flying as they are stacked with omelets, pancakes, waffles, bacon, ham, and cinnamon rolls. The scent of butter and bacon grease, mingled with gravy and freshly baked biscuits would intoxicate even the most disinterested bystander.

While breakfast is happening and lunch is prepared, the dishwasher begins to clean the huge vats that held sausage gravy, pot gravy, chipped beef gravy, and so on. The potato guy is also busy at his station, which has a Hobart potato peeler that shakes the skins off the potatoes, for the most part. The potato guy then has to go through and cut out any bad spot, or eyes, or places the machine did not quite catch. A raw, earthy potato scent fills that corner of the kitchen.

All breakfast dishes are made to order, so things can get pretty hectic. On this day, in the middle of a normal breakfast, the restaurant has suddenly received a group of thirty who are celebrating a christening. The salad lady, the cook, and the kitchen manager all jump in to help fill the influx of orders.

At one point, Michael rolls up his sleeves and cuts potatoes for home fries. "You have to be willing to do everything," he says.

Tammy, the kitchen manager, whose hands are red and raw, is also doing a little bit of everything all at once. At one point she looks up and says, "You've got to be a little strange to be in this business. I love it. It's the adrenalin rush, or something."

While Tammy and others are running around like crazy trying to get breakfast out, the waitresses come in to the kitchen and check on their orders. Tempers are high—and a few choice words are yelled back and forth between the waitresses and the kitchen staff. The waitresses want to keep their customers happy and the kitchen is working as fast as it can.

The servers have a standard to uphold; they need to be friendly and polite as well as professional. They are on the front line and must keep customers content, navigate the kitchen help, remember who needs what at which table, and be technically savvy enough to operate the computer ordering system. Even though this restaurant indeed has the feel of a grandmother's kitchen, it is run with cutting-edge technology that transmits information from the servers to the kitchen to the cashier and even upstairs to the manager's office for reporting purposes.

"Mother knew how to operate our first computer system. This new one is more complicated and she never did learn it. But she had the prices memorized and would figure it all out in her head. She knew that a dozen cookies cost a certain price and would add the taxes and everything. She'd collect the cash, put it in the register, and keep a running tab next to the register, and in her head," says Michael.

Rowe's has certainly changed from the early days when the family lived below the restaurant. It now has five walk-in freezers, upstairs and downstairs. Almost the entire basement is storage, except for the two rooms that Willard, Mildred, and the children lived in. These are the designated break rooms. And the bathroom that the family shared with their customers is still there. Also downstairs is the machine used to package Rowe's line of frozen entrées and a freezer for their storage. This line of retail goods is part of Brenda and Michael's legacy to the restaurant. The rest is pretty much all Mildred.

At this time, a month or so after her death, all of the seventy-five staff had at least met Mildred. Most of them knew her for fifteen to twenty-five or even thirty years. The business started with six employees. It's hard to imagine a time when most of the staff and customers will never have known the woman whose life force created this place. But it will happen.

Going forward, the staff and customers will certainly know Michael, who learned a lot from his mother and, after all, is very much like her. And they will know Aaron—the heir apparent.

Aaron seems content. The other employees say he is fun to work with and pulls his share of the load. He humbly says he still has a great deal to learn. But when this tall, striking young man walks into the kitchen with a quiet air of confidence, the air bristles. His coworkers' respect shows in their straightened postures, their more focused stance. Aaron doesn't notice the way they look at him. Michael cannot help but proud of his son's interest in the restaurant. Mildred was more than proud of him.

When Michael speaks of the future of the restaurant, he talks of adding another layer to the menu. He doesn't want to change the basic philosophy behind the food but would like to add some items that might appeal to a younger clientele.

He is also very carefully thinking about a transition in their marketing to a "next generation" focus. "This will always be Mother's place and there will always be a focus on that. But we also need to shift it a little to Aaron and myself."

As Mike tries to establish a new marketing plan and slightly revised menu, he will be taking over—more so than before—the host role, moving through the dining room and chatting with customers, making sure everything is as good as it can be. In the meantime, his son will be in the kitchen, learning everything he can. This line of continuity is a real comfort to the family.

Mildred always felt that as long as family was involved in the business, it would do well. She believed that they should not open another restaurant somewhere else for that very reason. In true Mildred Rowe fashion, she once said in a local newspaper article: "You got to be able to keep an eye on things." And perhaps she still is.

Mildred died in her sleep on Monday, January 13, 2003. Three days later, the day of her memorial service was cold and gray. It was as if someone had ordered the weather in Staunton to match the mood of the town. It was eerie to drive past

The day after Mildred's death,
Michael dreamed the most vivid dream he had ever
had. He was standing on a long, straight dirt road with
cornfields on either side. A little girl came walking
out of the fields. She was barefoot and happily playing
with butterflies that were swarming around her. She
was skipping, or doing something with her feet, and
she came up to Michael and looked at him. She seemed
very happy. She moved on down the road as he watched.
At the end of the road were two people,
a man and a woman, who took her hands
and they walked off together.
Michael knew the little girl was his mother.

Mrs. Rowe's Restaurant and Bakery, which was completely empty that morning so that her staff could attend the service.

The Saint Paul's United Methodist Church parking lot was full at 10:30 A.M.—a half hour before the service was supposed to start. The crowd consisted of white-haired women and men, middle-aged folks, young people, white people, and black people. More than six hundred family and friends crowded into the church.

The crowd sang her favorite old standards, "The Old Rugged Cross," "Amazing Grace," and "How Great Thou Art." Her grandchildren spoke about her. People cried and more important, they laughed and celebrated a life well-lived, full of complexity but also joy and success.

Mildred in the late 1990s, still going strong.

Imagine where she began—the little white farmhouse, surrounded by her mother's dahlias. The cornfields of Rich Patch. The days of horse and carriage glazed over by cars, electricity, and running water. A wide-eyed Mildred storming the factories and shops of Covington. A world-weary, wisecracking Mildred launching into the restaurant business in Goshen. Her hands scrubbing the "high-tech" golden laminate counter in the Far-Famed. Picking blackberries in Goshen. Standing next to Willard Rowe in front of Reverend H. G. Craig.

As a child in Rich Patch, if she had made wishes on the stars, they would have been simple—good crops in the summer, food for the winter, and a warm, comfortable place to sleep. And had she allowed herself to think of the distant future, she would have thought of a husband and children and maybe a farm of her own. Some things worked out for her better than she could possibly have imagined.

If there was a formula to Mildred's success, it would be grounded in hard work, and fueled by passion. Other keys were her honesty and integrity. She did not strive to be a restaurant owner; she simply saw an opportunity where she was and made the venture blossom. She did not have to move to New York or California to become an astounding success; she did not even have to go to cooking or business school. She took what she learned growing up in her mother's kitchen, along with what she learned from the wonderful cooks that worked for her, and forged a successful business. She listened to her own instincts and built on her native intelligence.

Humbled when asked what the secret to her success was, she once said, "I've thought about that for a long time. I guess if you like the food here, you just keep coming back."

Index

A

Alabama Biscuits, 5
Angel Biscuits, 6
Apples
    Apple Brown Betty, 187
    Apple Dumplings, 188–89
    Apple Pie, 147
    Baked Apples, 90
    B. B.'s Fried Apple Butter Pies, 190
    Black Walnut–Apple Pound Cake, 170
    Cheese and Cream Apple Pie, 150
    Fresh Apple Cake with Caramel Sauce, 175
    Fried Green Apples, 98
    Hot Applesauce Cake, 177
    Mincemeat Pie, 153
Aunt Sissy's Chocolate Cake, 168
Austin, Gladys and Sonie, 85

B

Baked Apples, 90
Baked Beans, 90
Baked Macaroni and Cheese, 91
Baked Pork Tenderloin and Gravy, 113
Baked Pork Tenderloin with Carrots and
    Mushrooms, 114
Baked Stuffed Pork Chops, 115
Baked Tomatoes, 92
Bananas
    Banana-Nut Bread, 10
    Banana Pudding, 191
    Virginia's Banana Pudding, 190
Barbecue Short Ribs, 116
B. B.'s Coleslaw and Dressing, 51
B. B.'s Fried Apple Butter Pies, 190
Beans
    Baked Beans, 90
    Black-Eyed Peas and Greens, 93
    Green Beans, 99
    Ham and Bean Soup, 68
    Succotash, 102
    White Beans, 103
    Willard's Brunswick Stew, 73

Beef
    Barbecue Short Ribs, 116
    Beef Liver and Onions, 126
    Chicken-Fried Steak, 118
    Chili, 74
    Chipped Beef Gravy, 35
    Country-Style Steak and Gravy, 121
    DiGrassie's Spaghetti Sauce, 28
    Mildred's Original Meatloaf, 127
    Mincemeat Pie, 153
    Old-Fashioned Beef Stew, 72
    Perk's Beef Stew, 75
    Pot Roast with Vegetables and Gravy, 130
    Short Rib Sauce, 30
    Stuffed Green Peppers, 134
    Vegetable Beef Soup, 69
Beets, Pickled, 59
Best-Ever Pound Cake, 169
Beverly Restaurant, 166–67
Biscuits
    Alabama Biscuits, 5
    Angel Biscuits, 6
    Buttermilk Biscuits, 7
    Creamed Turkey on Biscuits, 122
Blackberries
    Blackberry Jam, 37
    Blackberry Jam Cake with Caramel Icing,
        171
Black-Eyed Peas and Greens, 93
Black Walnut–Apple Pound Cake, 170
Blueberry Crisp with Old-Fashioned Lemon
    Sauce, 192
Boiled Cabbage, 93
Boiled Custard, 193
Bowers, Virginia Craft, 2–4, 19, 20, 181, 190
Bread
    Banana-Nut Bread, 10
    Bread Pudding with Raisin Sauce, 194
    Cherry Bread, 11
    Creamed Eggs on Toast, 17
    French Toast, 17
    Milk Toast, 16

Bread, *continued*
>   Pineapple Bread Pudding with Vanilla
>   Custard Sauce, 195
>   Skillet Cornbread, 12
>   Willard's Cornbread, 12
Bread and Butter Pickles, 57
Breakfast Tenderloin and Gravy, 117
Brown, Beverly, 34
Brown, Fred, 86, 88
Brownstone Front Cake, 172
Brown Sugar Pound Cake, 173
Brunswick Stew, Willard's, 73
Buttermilk
>   Buttermilk Biscuits, 7
>   Buttermilk Icing, 180
>   Buttermilk Pie, 148
Butterscotch Pie, 149

C

Cabbage
>   B. B.'s Coleslaw and Dressing, 51
>   Boiled Cabbage, 93
>   Chow-Chow, 58
>   Caesar Salad Dressing, 55
Cakes
>   Aunt Sissy's Chocolate Cake, 168
>   Best-Ever Pound Cake, 169
>   Blackberry Jam Cake with Caramel
>   Icing, 171
>   Black Walnut–Apple Pound Cake, 170
>   Brownstone Front Cake, 172
>   Brown Sugar Pound Cake, 173
>   Cranberry Cake, 174
>   Fresh Apple Cake with Caramel
>   Sauce, 175
>   Hot Applesauce Cake, 177
>   Mandarin Orange Cake, 178
>   Mildred's Fresh Coconut Cake, 176
>   Pineapple Pound Cake, 179
>   Prune Cake, 180
>   Vanilla Wafer Cake, 181

Candied Yams, 97
Canning instructions, 61
Caramel
>   Caramel Icing, 171, 172
>   Caramel Sauce, 175
Catfish, Fried, 123
Cheese
>   Baked Macaroni and Cheese, 91
>   Cheese and Cream Apple Pie, 150
>   Scalloped Tomatoes, 100
>   Squash Casserole, 101
Cherries
>   Cherry Bread, 11
>   Cherry Preserves, 37
Chicken
>   Chicken Noodle Soup, 70
>   Chicken Potpie, 119
>   Country-Style Chicken, 120
>   Fried Chicken Livers, 124
>   Old-Fashioned Chicken and
>   Dumplings, 128
>   Oven-Broiled Barbecue Chicken, 129
>   Southern Fried Chicken, 133
>   Willard's Brunswick Stew, 73
>   Chicken-Fried Steak, 118
>   Chili, 74
Chipped Beef Gravy, 35
Chocolate
>   Aunt Sissy's Chocolate Cake, 168
>   Aunt Sissy's Chocolate Icing, 168
>   Brownstone Front Cake, 172
>   Chocolate Meringue Pie, 151
>   Never-Fail Fudge, 196
>   Pecan–Chocolate Chunk Cookies, 198
Chow-Chow, 58
Clemmer, Frances, 108
Clemmer, Frank, 126
Cocktail Sauce, 27
Coconut
>   Fresh Apple Cake with Caramel
>   Sauce, 175
>   Mildred's Fresh Coconut Cake, 176
>   Original Coconut Cream Pie, 155
>   Vanilla Wafer Cake, 181
Coleslaw and Dressing, B. B.'s, 51

Cookies
    Oatmeal Raisin Cookies, 197
    Pecan–Chocolate Chunk Cookies, 198
Corn
    Chicken or Turkey Potpie, 119
    Corn Pudding, 94
    Creamed Corn, 95
    Creamed Turkey on Biscuits, 122
    Succotash, 102
    Willard's Brunswick Stew, 73
    Cornmeal
    Skillet Cornbread, 12
    Spoon Bread, 13
    Spoon Bread Soufflé, 14
    Willard's Cornbread, 12
Country Cooked Greens, 96
Country-Style Chicken, 120
Country-Style Steak and Gravy, 121
Covington, Virginia, 19, 21, 25
Craft, Bobby, 64
Craft, James Henry, 2, 41, 64
Craft, John, Jr., 3
Craft, Ruth Ann, 1, 2
Craig, Karl, 31, 79
Cranberry Cake, 174
Creamed Corn, 95
Creamed Eggs on Toast, 17
Creamed Turkey on Biscuits, 122
Cream of Potato and Bacon Soup, 71
Crisp, Blueberry, with Old-Fashioned Lemon
    Sauce, 192
Cronk, Clara, 155
Cucumbers
    Bread and Butter Pickles, 57
    Cucumbers and Onions, 50
Custard
    Boiled Custard, 193
    Old-Fashioned Egg Custard Pie, 154
    Vanilla Custard Sauce, 195

D

Davis, Agnes, 43
DiGrassie, Aaron
    in the kitchen, xxiv, 35, 117, 144, 188,
      201, 203

recipes of, 78, 79, 114
recollections by, xv, 34, 69, 172
DiGrassie, Eugene, xvii, 22–26, 39, 42, 46,
    49, 142
DiGrassie, Michael
    childhood of, 41, 42, 45, 65, 66, 70, 105–6,
      107, 139
    at college, 140, 141–42
    recollections by, 28, 36, 41, 50, 53, 54, 66,
      70, 71, 72, 99, 112, 132, 153
    at the restaurant, xxiii, 144, 151, 164–66,
      167, 202, 203–4
DiGrassie's Grille, 42, 45, 48
DiGrassie's Spaghetti Sauce, 28
Dill Tomatoes, 59
Dumplings
    Apple Dumplings, 188–89
    Old-Fashioned Chicken and
      Dumplings, 128

E

Eggs
    Creamed Eggs on Toast, 17
    Old-Fashioned Egg Custard Pie, 154
Ever, Rudolph, 167
Ever's Country Buffet, 167

F

Far-Famed, 45, 48, 65, 86, 91, 128
Finley, Anne, 144
Fish
    Fried Catfish, 123
    Salmon Cakes with White Sauce, 131
French Toast, 17
Fresh Apple Cake with Caramel Sauce, 175
Fried Catfish, 123
Fried Chicken Livers, 124
Fried Green Apples, 98
Fried Green Tomatoes, 98
Fried Oysters, 125
Fruit. *See also individual fruits*
    Millionaire Pie, 196
Fudge, Never-Fail, 196
Fultz, Betsy, 30, 91, 116

G

Glazes
    Orange Glaze, 174
    Pineapple Glaze, 179
Goshen, Virginia, 39–49
Graham, Mary-Lydia, 93
Grasty, Phil, 126
Gravies
    Chicken-Fried Steak Gravy, 118
    Chipped Beef Gravy, 35
    Pot Gravy, 35
    Sausage Gravy, 34
Green Beans, 99
Greens
    Black-Eyed Peas and Greens, 93
    Country Cooked Greens, 96

H

Ham
    Green Beans, 99
    Ham and Bean Soup, 68
    Virginia Country Ham with Redeye
      Gravy, 135
    White Beans, 103
Hamilton, Geneva, 164
Hanna, Linda DiGrassie, 28, 42, 89, 107–8,
    112, 140, 150, 169, 193
Harner, Jean, xiv, 87
Harner, Marion, xiv, 138
Harrison, Sarah, 141, 143, 166
Hathaway, Brenda
    childhood of, 23, 42, 46, 89, 106, 107, 139
    recollections by, 17, 29, 49, 58, 77, 132, 189
    at the restaurant, xxiv, 140–44, 164–65, 203
Hilt, Sue, 164
Hinkle, Annie, xx, xxii, 45
Hinton, Carole, 164
The Homestead, 22, 25
Hot Applesauce Cake, 177
Hot Dogs, Fried, Potato Soup with, 77
Hot Rolls, 8
Hutching-Mass, Sissy, xx

I

Icings
    Aunt Sissy's Chocolate Icing, 168
    Buttermilk Icing, 180
    Caramel Icing, 171, 172

J

Jams. *See* Preserves
Jaquith, Edie, 127
Jarret, Danie, 86

K

Klotz family, 110

L

Landes, Junior, 88
LeMasurier, Ginger Rowe, 9, 105–8, 110, 111,
    137–39, 150
Lemons
    Lemon Meringue Pie, 152
    Old-Fashioned Lemon Sauce, 192
Limes
    Lime Pickles, 60
    Sweet Lime Pickles, 60
Liver
    Beef Liver and Onions, 126
    Fried Chicken Livers, 124

M

Macaroni and Cheese, Baked, 91
Mandarin oranges
    Mandarin Orange Cake, 178
    Mandarin Orange Salad, 52
Marshall, Barbara, 13
Mays, Basil, 39, 41, 42, 43, 46, 85
Mays, Bertha Craft
    life of, 19, 20, 39, 41, 42, 43, 85, 106
    recipes of, 5–7, 14, 51, 53, 54, 190
    recollections by, 2, 3, 46, 63, 82
Mays, Carroll, xvi, 39, 42, 64–65, 173
McLear, Tootie, xxiii, 88, 164

Meatloaf, Mildred's Original, 127
Medium White Sauce, 32
Meringues
    Mrs. Rowe's Meringue, 146
    Weepless Meringue, 146
Mildred's Fresh Coconut Cake, 176
Mildred's Original Meatloaf, 127
Milk Toast, 16
Mill Creek Cafe, 48, 67
Millionaire Pie, 196
Mincemeat Pie, 153
Morris, John, 72, 92, 106
Morris, Reba, 86
Mrs. Rowe's Meringue, 146
Mrs. Rowe's Restaurant and Bakery
    atmosphere of, xv–xvi, 163, 186, 201–2
    expansions of, 164–66
    future of, 203–4
    number of meals served by, xix
    popular dishes at, xxi
    success of, xix, xx, xxii–xxiii
Muffins
    Orange Blossoms, 9
Mushrooms
    Baked Pork Tenderloin with Carrots and
        Mushrooms, 114
    DiGrassie's Spaghetti Sauce, 28

N

Never-Fail Fudge, 196
Noodles
    Baked Macaroni and Cheese, 91
    Chicken Noodle Soup, 70

O

Oatmeal Raisin Cookies, 197
Obie, Vivian, 191
Old-Fashioned Beef Stew, 72
Old-Fashioned Chicken and Dumplings, 128
Old-Fashioned Egg Custard Pie, 154
Old-Fashioned Lemon Sauce, 192

Onions
    Beef Liver and Onions, 126
    Cucumbers and Onions, 50
    Sweet Onion Soup, 78
Oranges. See also Mandarin oranges
    Orange Blossoms, 9
    Orange Glaze, 174
Original Coconut Cream Pie, 155
Oven-Broiled Barbecue Chicken, 129
Oyster George, xxiv
Oysters
    Fried Oysters, 125
    Willard's Sunday Oyster Stew, 76

P

Pancakes
    Pumpkin-Pecan Pancakes, 15
    Rowe's Regular Pancakes, 16
Paxton, John, 39
Peanut Butter Pie, 156
Pecans
    Banana-Nut Bread, 10
    Cherry Bread, 11
    Cranberry Cake, 174
    Pecan–Chocolate Chunk Cookies, 198
    Pecan Puffs, 199
    Prune Cake, 180
    Pumpkin-Pecan Pancakes, 15
    Southern Pecan Pie, 161
    Vanilla Wafer Cake, 181
Peppers, Stuffed Green, 134
Perk's Barbecue, 75, 81, 84, 85, 88–89
Perk's Beef Stew, 75
Pickles
    Bread and Butter Pickles, 57
    canning instructions for, 61
    Chow-Chow, 58
    Lime Pickles, 60
    Pickled Beets, 59
    Sweet Lime Pickles, 60
Pie crusts
    Plain Pie Pastry, 145
    Vinegar Pie Crust, 145

Pies. *See also* Meringues; Pie crusts
    Apple Pie, 147
    B. B.'s Fried Apple Butter Pies, 190
    Buttermilk Pie, 148
    Butterscotch Pie, 149
    Cheese and Cream Apple Pie, 150
    Chocolate Meringue Pie, 151
    Lemon Meringue Pie, 152
    Mincemeat Pie, 153
    Old-Fashioned Egg Custard Pie, 154
    Original Coconut Cream Pie, 155
    Peanut Butter Pie, 156
    Pineapple Cream Pie, 157
    Pineapple Meringue Pie, 158
    Rhubarb Pie, 159
    Southern Pecan Pie, 161
    Strawberry-Rhubarb Pie, 160
Pineapple
    Mandarin Orange Cake, 178
    Pineapple Bread Pudding with Vanilla
        Custard Sauce, 195
    Pineapple Cream Pie, 157
    Pineapple Glaze, 179
    Pineapple Meringue Pie, 158
    Pineapple Pound Cake, 179
Plain Pie Pastry, 145
Pork
    Baked Pork Tenderloin and Gravy, 113
    Baked Pork Tenderloin with Carrots and
        Mushrooms, 114
    Baked Stuffed Pork Chops, 115
    Breakfast Tenderloin and Gravy, 117
    Pork Barbecue, 129
    Pork Barbecue Sauce, 29
    Willard's Brunswick Stew, 73
Potatoes
    Cream of Potato and Bacon Soup, 71
    Old-Fashioned Beef Stew, 72
    Perk's Beef Stew, 75
    Potato Salad, 53
    Potato Soup with Fried Hot Dogs, 77
    Pot Roast with Vegetables and Gravy, 130
    Willard's Brunswick Stew, 73
Pot Gravy, 35
Potpie, Chicken or Turkey, 119

Pot Roast with Vegetables and Gravy, 130
Preserves
    Blackberry Jam, 37
    Cherry Preserves, 37
    Raspberry Jam, 37
    Strawberry Preserves, 36
Prune Cake, 180
Puddings
    Banana Pudding, 191
    Bread Pudding with Raisin Sauce, 194
    Corn Pudding, 94
    Pineapple Bread Pudding with Vanilla
        Custard Sauce, 195
    Virginia's Banana Pudding, 190
    Pumpkin-Pecan Pancakes, 15

R

Raisins
    Apple Brown Betty, 187
    Banana-Nut Bread, 10
    Fresh Apple Cake with Caramel Sauce,
        175
    Hot Applesauce Cake, 177
    Mincemeat Pie, 153
    Oatmeal Raisin Cookies, 197
    Pineapple Bread Pudding with Vanilla
        Custard Sauce, 195
    Raisin Sauce, 194
Ramps, 64
Raspberry Jam, 37
Reiner, Wynne DiGrassie, 121, 188
Rhubarb
    Rhubarb Pie, 159
    Strawberry-Rhubarb Pie, 160
Rich Patch, Virginia, 1–4, 19–20
Robertson, Marion, 89, 112
Rolls, Hot, 8
Rowe, Clara, 128, 129
Rowe, Mildred Craft
    birth of, 1, 2
    childhood of, 1, 2–4
    during the Depression, 19–20
    marries Eugene DiGrassie, 22–26
    in Goshen, 39–49, 63–67
    meets and marries Willard, 66, 67, 81–85

in Staunton, 84, 86–87, 89, 105–12, 137
on death of Willard, 139–40
runs restaurant with her children,
    140–44, 164–66, 202, 203–4
death of, 204
memorial service for, xxiv–xxv, 204–5
berry picking and, 64–65
church and, 111–12
compassion of, xxii
as driver, 19–20
as gardener, 63, 99
as golfer, 166
grandchildren of, 183
horses and, 111
personality of, xv, xvii–xviii, 89, 137, 163–
    64, 183–86
success of, xx, xxii–xxiii, xxiv, 164, 206
as traveler, 166
Rowe, Willard
    childhood of, 87
    Perk's Barbecue and, 88–89
    meets and marries Mildred, xx, 66, 67,
        81–85
Rowe's Seafood and Steakhouse and, 86–87,
    107, 138–39
    illness and death of, 139–40
    cars of, 66, 87
    cleanliness of, 87
    favorite dishes of, 16, 76, 125
    recipes of, 12, 29, 56, 73, 102, 129, 157
Rowe's Regular Pancakes, 16
Rowe's Seafood and Steakhouse, 84, 86,
    105, 108

S

Salad dressings
    Caesar Salad Dressing, 55
    Willard's Thousand Island Dressing, 56
Salads
    B. B.'s Coleslaw and Dressing, 51
    Cucumbers and Onions, 50
    Mandarin Orange Salad, 52
    Potato Salad, 53
    Sauerkraut Salad, 54
Salmon Cakes with White Sauce, 131

Sauces
    Caramel Sauce, 175
    Cocktail Sauce, 27
    DiGrassie's Spaghetti Sauce, 28
    Medium White Sauce, 32
    Old-Fashioned Lemon Sauce, 192
    Pork Barbecue Sauce, 29
    Raisin Sauce, 194
    Short Rib Sauce, 30
    Stuffed Pepper Sauce, 134
    Sweet and Sour Sauce, 31
    Tartar Sauce, 27
    Thick White Sauce, 33
    Thin White Sauce, 32
    Vanilla Custard Sauce, 195
Sauerkraut Salad, 54
Sausage Gravy, 34
Sawyer, Barb, 166
Sawyer, John, 111, 112
Scalloped Tomatoes, 100
Shimer, Bill, 115
Short Rib Sauce, 30
Skillet Cornbread, 12
Soufflé, Spoon Bread, 14
Soups
    Chicken Noodle Soup, 70
    Cream of Potato and Bacon Soup, 71
    Ham and Bean Soup, 68
    Potato Soup with Fried Hot Dogs, 77
    Sweet Onion Soup, 78
    Tomato-Basil Soup, 79
    Vegetable Beef Soup, 69
Southern Fried Chicken, 133
Southern Pecan Pie, 161
Spoon Bread, 13
Spoon Bread Soufflé, 14
Squash Casserole, 101
Squirrel and Gravy, 132
Staunton, Virginia, 82, 86, 105–10
Stern, Jane and Michael, 142–43, 191
Stews
    Old-Fashioned Beef Stew, 72
    Perk's Beef Stew, 75
    Willard's Brunswick Stew, 73
    Willard's Sunday Oyster Stew, 76

Stoner, Rod, 185
Strawberries
    Strawberry Preserves, 36
    Strawberry-Rhubarb Pie, 160
Stuffed Green Peppers, 134
Succotash, 102
Sweet and Sour Sauce, 31
Sweet Lime Pickles, 60
Sweet Onion Soup, 78

T

Tartar Sauce, 27
Terry, Juanita, 65
Thick White Sauce, 33
Thin White Sauce, 32
Thomas, Janet and Paul, 166–67
Thompson, Lorraine, 43
Thompson, Roscoe, 54
Thousand Island Dressing, Willard's, 56
Tomatoes
    Baked Tomatoes, 92
    Chow-Chow, 58
    DiGrassie's Spaghetti Sauce, 28
    Dill Tomatoes, 59
    Fried Green Tomatoes, 98
    Ham and Bean Soup, 68
    Perk's Beef Stew, 75
    Scalloped Tomatoes, 100
    Tomato-Basil Soup, 79
    Vegetable Beef Soup, 69
    Willard's Brunswick Stew, 73
Turkey
    Creamed Turkey on Biscuits, 122
    Turkey Potpie, 119
Turner, Sheila, 164

V

Vanilla Custard Sauce, 195
Vanilla wafers
    Banana Pudding, 191
    Vanilla Wafer Cake, 181
Virginia's Banana Pudding, 190
Vegetable Beef Soup, 69
Vinegar Pie Crust, 145

Virginia Country Ham with Redeye Gravy, 135
Virginia's Banana Pudding, 190

W

Walker, Edgar, 41, 48
Walnuts
    Blackberry Jam Cake with Caramel
      Icing, 171
    Black Walnut–Apple Pound Cake, 170
    Brown Sugar Pound Cake, 173
    Cranberry Cake, 174
    Fresh Apple Cake with Caramel
      Sauce, 175
    Hot Applesauce Cake, 177
    Never-Fail Fudge, 196
Weepless Meringue, 146
White Beans, 103
Wilkins, Whitney, 184
Willard's Brunswick Stew, 73
Willard's Cornbread, 12
Willard's Sunday Oyster Stew, 76
Willard's Thousand Island Dressing, 56
Wing Dings, 133
Woodrum, Dot, 151

Y

Yams, Candied, 97